It's Fast, It's Easy, It's Delicious and . . .

It's Microwaved!

by
Caralan Dams, B.Sc. (H.Ec.)
and
Susan VanderVelde

It's Microwaved!
by
Caralan Dams, B.Sc. (H.Ec.)
Susan VanderVelde

First Printing — June, 1985
Second Printing — September, 1985

Canadian Cataloguing in Publication Data

Dams, Caralan, 1956-
  It's microwaved

Includes index.
ISBN 0-919845-30-4.

1. Microwave cookery. I. VanderVelde, Susan, 1948-
II. Title.
TX832.D35 1985   641.5'882   C85-091271-7

Photography by:
Peter Bolli
Bolli & Hutchinson Photographic Design Ltd.
Calgary, Alberta

Dishes and Accessories courtesy of:
The Bay, Calgary
Brandi's Kitchen Boutique Ltd., Calgary
Import Bazaar, Calgary

Corning Canada Inc. generously donated
   Corning Ware cookware, Corelle Livingware, Pyrex ovenware
Toshiba of Canada Ltd. provided use of their microwave oven.

Designed, Printed and Produced in Canada by
Centax of Canada
Publishing Consultant and Food Stylist — Margo Embury
Design by Blair Fraser
1048 Fleury Street
Regina, Saskatchewan, Canada   S4N 4W8
(306) 359-3737

#105 - 4711 13 Street N.E.
Calgary, Alberta, Canada   T2E 6M3

Dedicated With Love
to our Children

Brad and Carrie

Jeff and Marty

With Thanks

We wish to thank our families, friends and many students who encouraged us to write "It's Microwaved". Our families have been a tremendous support and deserve our deepest gratitude. In particular, we wish to thank Mr. and Mrs. E. Dancoine (Susan's parents), and Mr. and Mrs. Bob Murray (Caralan's parents) for their continued love, support, and encouragement.

Many thanks to our relatives, and good friends who were kind enough to share their most treasured recipes with us. Margo Embury of Centax, Canada has also been a terrific help to us in the final stages of the manuscript preparation and food photography.

A special thank you to the administration staff of Intera Technologies Ltd. for their patience, cooperation and support.

A final, but most important thanks goes to our husbands, Bob Dams and Allan VanderVelde who have seen us through this from start to finish; they were always there for us when we needed advice, encouragement and support. "It's Microwaved" would not have been possible without them!

Tribute To Microwave Cooks

The eggs blew up, and the sauce turned to glue
Surely this contraption is not for you!
You've tried to cook with color and appeal,
But the family still say grace after the meal!

Husband dear, look what you've done!
You've rubberized this hamburger bun.
Get this microwave out of my kitchen,
You've got to be tired of my constant witchen.

You've had your oven for just a short time
And the response from the family isn't worth a dime
Each day you're ready, willing and able,
So what if Rover no longer begs at your table!

If at first you don't succeed,
Don't stamp your feet, holler and plead.
Don't give up and don't despair,
Our recipes and hints we will be happy to share,

If the recipes you've tried aren't quite fit for a King,
This book is the answer to everything.
Our years of testing, our trials and tribulations
Are in this book for our friends and relations.

Get on that apron, and open this book,
Turn to page 20 and have a look!
It's easy, it's fast and lots of fun
And before you know it, the cookin' is done!

Susan VanderVelde

Table of Contents

Notes From the Authors:

So you want to do more than warm your coffee and heat left-overs in your microwave oven? Are you ready for some innovative ideas? This book is the answer! It represents a combined sixteen years of teaching experience, coupled with years of recipe testing.

"It's Microwaved" is unique and exciting; it includes helpful hints, crafts and over 200 splendid recipes. We have assembled for you a collection of recipes to suit your every need. Each recipe is clear and concise with respect to ingredients, quantities and methods.

A common problem with microwave cooking is establishing proper cooking times and power levels. We have presented a range of times, a suggested power level and a description indicating doneness. For example, "Microwave pork on MEDIUM HIGH for 4-6 minutes, or until it is no longer pink". It is important to realize that suggested times are approximate, there are many variables that affect total cooking times. Always start with the minimum time and increase time gradually as needed. In addition, always undercook food slightly, it will continue to cook after removal from the microwave.

Power levels have been expressed as follows: HIGH, MEDIUM HIGH, MEDIUM and LOW. Some manufacturers use different terminology when referring to power levels. If your oven has settings that differ from the above, please refer to the following chart:

POWER LEVEL CHART

Setting	Approximate % of power
HIGH	100%
MEDIUM HIGH	70%
MEDIUM	50%
LOW	30%

The recipes in the book have been tested on a 700 watt output oven. If your oven output differs, (the wattage will be on the back of your microwave) you may have to adjust your cooking times slightly. For a 600-650 watt oven, you may find longer cooking time more appropriate. For more than a 720 watt oven you may find shorter cooking times appropriate. Remember you are the final judge of doneness. Timings given in this book are only a guideline. Our descriptions of how a food should look at any given step in the recipe will help to prevent confusion when determining the proper cooking times.

 The number in the MINI MICROWAVE refers to one of our handy hints which are given on pages 8 through 12. You will find it useful to read all of our hints for some have not been referred to in the recipe section.

Please let us know if you have any comments, suggestions or questions. Above all, we are confident that you will be able to prepare and serve a meal and be proud to say "Yes, IT'S MICROWAVED!"

COOK

POWER
LEVEL

TIME

1	2	3
4	5	6
7	8	9
0		CLEAR

START

POWER LEVEL

Brainwaves and Quick Recipes

1. Microwave cooking times are affected by many variables, two very important variables are the amount and depth of food in the dish. If you decrease or increase the recipe size, you must also change your timing. Decrease time by ⅓ when halving a recipe, and add ½ to ⅔ more microwave time when doubling a recipe. Use a dish that is deep enough to prevent foods from boiling over and wide enough to keep the depth of the food the same as the original recipe.

2. No two microwave ovens cook at the same speed. During peak periods of power consumption your oven may not cook as fast as at other times. This explains why recipes are written with a range of microwave cooking times (e.g., microwave on HIGH for 4-6 minutes). Always microwave the minimum time suggested, check the food for doneness, and then add extra time if it is required. Do not forget to allow for some carry-over cooking time, and ALWAYS undercook food slightly. Food will continue its cooking process while standing.

3. If your microwave does not come with a probe, you can use a conventional thermometer, immediately after removing the meat, casserole, etc. from the microwave. DO NOT USE A CONVENTIONAL THERMOMETER INSIDE THE MICROWAVE. Insert the tip of the thermometer into the center of the meat. Let stand 1 minute and check the internal temperature. If the internal temperature has not reached the desired degree of doneness, microwave additional time as needed, after removing the thermometer.

4. Microwaving extracts more fat from meats than conventional cooking methods do (great for dieters!). It is important that you drain all meats after cooking them in the microwave, especially if you plan to add a sauce to the meat, or if you plan to add the meat to a casserole.

5. Pork chops should be cooked in a sauce, in a covered casserole and microwaved on MEDIUM. If other cooking methods are used, the chops tend to toughen and dry out.

6. Meats such as ground beef, chicken or ham should be partially cooked in the microwave BEFORE adding glazes and sauces. Glazes and sauces generally have high fat and sugar content which may cause burning. The meat itself will also take longer to cook if sauces are added before the meat is partially cooked. Sauces should be added during the last few minutes of cooking time.

7. Vegetables in hard shells or tight skins such as turnips, pumpkin, sweet potato, squash, etc. can be easily cooked in the microwave. These types of vegetables can be microwaved right in nature's jacket. It is not necessary to peel and cut these vegetables or add water. Skins should be pierced with a sharp knife and the vegetables placed in the microwave. They may be elevated for more even cooking. One medium turnip will require 8-10 minutes microwaving time on HIGH.

Brainwaves and Quick Recipes (cont'd)

8. Cook your squash for 5-7 minutes on HIGH, before you attempt to cut it open for stuffing etc. It is much easier to cut when partially cooked. After filling with butter, sugar, nuts, etc., continue to microwave on HIGH until the squash is fork-tender.

9. Toast coconut and almonds in the microwave quickly and easily. Microwave ½ cup (125 mL) of either, spread out on a plate, for ¾-1 minute, uncovered, on HIGH. Do not attempt to completely brown as the toasting process will continue during the standing time. Overcooking will scorch.

10. Make your own croutons for a fraction of the cost. Melt ¼ cup (50 mL) of butter, add ¼ tsp. (1 mL) each garlic powder and onion powder plus 1 tsp. (5 mL) dried parsley. Pour evenly over 2 cups (500 mL) of cubed bread which has been spread in a pie plate. Microwave uncovered for 2-3 minutes on HIGH. Stir frequently. Let stand 5-10 minutes to complete the drying and crisping process. Spices may be altered according to taste. See photograph page 48.

11. Soften hard ice cream for scooping. A 2-quart (2 L) brick of ice cream will soften on LOW in 1-1½ minutes. Decrease time as needed. Careful! Ice cream defrosts very quickly. Melted ice cream is a good substitute for cream on apple crisp or even in your coffee.

12. 1 cup (250 mL) frozen whipping cream can be defrosted on LOW, in 1-2 minutes. Let stand 2 minutes. Whip with electric beater. This allows you to buy whipping cream and freeze until needed.

13. Cheese can be brought to room temperature for a much fuller flavor. Microwave on LOW just until the cheese no longer feels cool to touch.

14. Extract more juice from lemons, limes and oranges by placing them in the microwave and microwaving on HIGH 30-45 seconds for each single piece of fruit.

15. Underripe avocados will ripen in a minute!!! Pierce skin once and microwave on HIGH 1 minute. Let stand 2 minutes before peeling. Add time in 30 second intervals as required to complete the softening if necessary.

16. To soften brown sugar, place a piece of bread on top of 2 cups (500 mL) of brown sugar in a casserole and cover with a heavy lid. Microwave on HIGH 1 minute. You may need to repeat at 1 minute intervals until sugar is softened.

17. Defrost half of that large package of hamburger, pork chops, hotdogs or bacon. Cover the portion of meat you DO NOT want defrosted with aluminum foil. DO NOT LET THE FOIL TOUCH THE SIDES OF THE OVEN! The exposed portion will defrost and the wrapped portion will stay frozen.
The general rule for using foil is to have MORE FOOD THAN FOIL MASS and keep the foil AT LEAST 1" (2.5 cm) FROM THE SIDES OF THE OVEN.

18. Warm brandy, saki or heat liqueur for flambéing. Microwave 1 oz. (25 mL) of liqueur for 20 seconds ON HIGH. Never boil alcohol.

Brainwaves and Quick Recipes (cont'd)

19. For a quick barbecue, precook chicken or roasts in the microwave and barbecue afterwards.
    Approximate timings for precooking:
    4 lb. (2 kg) chicken — 20 minutes, covered, on HIGH
    4 lb. (2 kg) pork roast — 30 minutes, covered, on MEDIUM
    4 lb. (2 kg) beef roast — 25 minutes, covered, on MEDIUM
    Pre-microwaving will prevent meat from burning on the outside BEFORE completely cooking on the inside, once it is on the barbecue.

20. Peaches and tomatoes will peel much more easily after being microwaved. Microwave each peach or tomato for 45 seconds. Do not pierce the skin. Let stand 1 minute before peeling.

21. Frozen fruit juice concentrates in cardboard cans may be defrosted quickly. The top of the can must be removed. Juice in metal cans cannot be defrosted in the microwave. The metallic painted cans will arc and spark and should not be put in the microwave. A 1 cup (250 mL) cardboard can of frozen juice will defrost when microwaved for 1-1½ minutes on HIGH.

22. Cook up a quick paté with chicken livers. Pierce skins before microwaving. Microwave 1 lb. (500 g) of chicken livers, covered on MEDIUM HIGH for 7-8 minutes or until they are no longer pink.

23. Melting chocolate is accomplished easily and quickly, with very little mess. Microwave 1 cup (250 mL) chocolate chips, uncovered, on MEDIUM for 2 minutes. 1 square of chocolate can be melted in its paper wrapper on MEDIUM for 1 minute. Stir any chocolate frequently when it is being microwaved as it does not lose its shape and it is difficult to establish doneness. Chocolate will scorch if overcooked.

24. When preparing appetizers, keep the crackers crispy by spreading the mixture on the crackers JUST BEFORE MICROWAVING.

25. Egg yolks contain a high fat content and attract more microwave energy than the whites. To avoid the problem of unevenly cooked eggs, microwave on MEDIUM for 50 seconds per egg. Always pierce whites and yolks with a fork before cooking. Add on 10-second intervals as needed, until the whites JUST become opaque. Let stand 1-2 minutes.

26. Precook the bottom pie shell BEFORE adding a filling, otherwise the pie crust will be soggy as it absorbs moisture from the filling. For a double crusted pie see page 126 for baking instructions.

27. Use your dinner plates in place of lids or plastic wrap. The steam from the food rises, heating your dinner plates. Covering any food also helps the food cook more quickly. Since microwave foods cool quickly it is great to eat from a heated plate. This also means a saving on expensive plastic wrap.

Brainwaves and Quick Recipes (cont'd)

28. For baked breads, scalloped potatoes, or any recipe calling for scalded milk, microwave 1 cup (250 mL) of milk on HIGH, uncovered 1½-2 minutes. Scald 2 cups (500 mL) of milk for 2½-3 minutes. Use a large measuring cup and eliminate those hard-to-clean pots and pans.

29. Although you cannot cook crêpes, waffles or pancakes in the microwave, you can easily reheat these foods. Reheat 4 frozen pancakes or waffles on HIGH 1½-2 minutes, 4 frozen crêpes on HIGH 1-1½ minutes.

30. Uncrystalize 2 cups (500 mL) of honey for 1½-2 minutes on HIGH, uncovered. Cover tightly after microwaving to keep honey soft.

31. To reheat frozen pizza, and to reduce the sogginess of the crust, place a piece of pizza on a microwave roasting rack, a paper towel, or a preheated browning dish. A microwave accessory called a pizza stone is also ideal for this.

32. Microwaved food does cool down more quickly! While microwaving, the heat from the food is drawn out by the coolness of the cooking container. This is especially noticeable with vegetables. To keep food warm, place the container in wicker serving basket, or wrap the container with a dish towel. Plastics manufactured for the microwave are a good alternative to glass because the food does not cool down as quickly in these containers.

33. Kebob recipes can easily be adapted for the microwave. Bamboo skewers should be used instead of the metal skewers. It is advisable to precook the meat before assembling the kebobs with the vegetables as meat requires a longer cooking time.

34. Frozen baked pies that are sold in foil containers can be defrosted in the microwave. Most pies will "pop out" of the pan and can then be carefully placed in a similar size glass pie plate. One double crusted fruit pie will defrost in 7-8 minutes on LOW.

35. If you do not have a microwave muffin pan, cut off the top half of paper or styrofoam cups and line with muffin paper. Arrange up to 8 muffins in a circle in the microwave and microwave on HIGH 20-30 seconds per muffin or until the muffin surfaces JUST lose their wet appearance.

36. Potato chips or crackers stale? Microwave 2 cups (500 mL) of any snack food, uncovered, on HIGH for 1 minute to instantly freshen.

37. Pork spareribs to be glazed or added to a sauce should be precooked first. To precook ribs, place in a casserole and cover with water. For every 1 lb. (.5 kg) of ribs, add ¼ cup (125 mL) of vinegar to the water. Microwave, covered, on HIGH for 5 minutes, then on MEDIUM for 7-10 minutes per lb. (.5 kg).

38. To make red and white wine vinegars combine equal portions of white/red wine and vinegar. What a great way to use up those leftover wines.

Brainwaves and Quick Recipes (cont'd)

39. Whip whipping cream ahead of time and place it in a strainer resting in a large bowl. This keeps the cream light and fluffy. The separated cream in the bottom of the bowl can be rewhipped or used as coffee cream. When making Irish coffee, whip the cream and pipe it onto a cookie sheet. Freeze until needed.

40. When removing a cup of boiling water from the microwave you may experience uneven heating whereby the water boils over when removing the mug from the oven. To prevent this, reach into the microwave and stir the water BEFORE removing the mug.

41. Place a 3-4 lb. (1.5-2 kg) chicken, breast side down, in a 1-2 qt. (1-2 L) casserole. Cover and microwave on HIGH 18-20 minutes. Cool and remove skin. Remove meat from bones and dice into bite-size pieces. Since this is so quick and easy to do, cook extra chicken as directed above and freeze to have on hand for sandwiches, crêpes, casseroles and quiche. Reserve broth and freeze for soups and sauces.

42. Bake potatoes faster and more evenly. Scrub the potatoes, leaving them slightly moist. Place 6 large potatoes in a casserole, cover with a heavy lid or 3 or 4 dinner plates and microwave on HIGH 15-18 minutes. Let stand 5 minutes. These potatoes can be used for potato salad, fried potatoes, peeled, mashed or stuffed, or even foil-wrapped and barbecued. This can also be done with a combination of potatoes, carrots and onions before wrapping in foil to barbecue.

43. For light fluffy rice, always wash the rice. To speed up the cooking, microwave rice with boiling water on MEDIUM. For every 1 cup (250 mL) white, converted rice use 2 cups (500 mL) boiling water, and microwave on MEDIUM 14-16 minutes. Let stand at least 5 minutes. For brown rice follow package instructions as per water proportions and microwave an additional 5-7 minutes.

44. When microwaving fish or seafood, cover with a lid, dinner plate, inverted pie plate or Saran Wrap.

45. Fish cooks rapidly. To avoid overcooking, check and rearrange fish after half the cooking time. The fish is done when it is opaque and flakes easily. It may still be translucent in the centre, however this will complete cooking after standing 2-3 minutes.

46. Whenever you have a recipe calling for sweetened condensed milk and none in the cupboard, this is a super substitute. Combine: 1½ cups (375 mL) white sugar, ⅔ cup (150 mL) water, ⅔ cup (150 mL) margarine, and 2 cups (500 mL) skim milk (do not substitute). Microwave, uncovered, on HIGH 5-7 minutes or until thickened.

COOK

POWER LEVEL

TIME

1	2	3
4	5	6
7	8	9
0		CLEAR

START

POWER LEVEL

Leprechaun's Delight!

1 cup	piping hot coffee	250 mL
1 oz.	orange brandy or Grand Marnier	25 mL
1 oz.	Irish Cream liqueur	25 mL
	whipped cream	
	grated orange rind	
1	leprechaun, optional	1

1. Stir brandy and liqueur into piping hot coffee. Top with a dollop of whipped cream and sprinkle with grated orange rind. Divide into 2 equal parts, 1 for you and 1 for the leprechaun.
   See photograph on front cover.

Kahlúa

2 cups	sugar	500 mL
2 cups	water	500 mL
1 cup	instant POWDERED coffee	250 mL
1 cup	water	250 mL
4 cups	vodka	1 L
1	vanilla bean	1
1 tsp.	glycerin, optional *	5 mL

1. Combine sugar and 2 cups water. Microwave on HIGH 3-5 minutes or until boiling. Continue to boil for 2 minutes. Set aside. Sugar should be completely dissolved.
2. Combine powdered coffee and 1 cup water. Microwave, uncovered, on HIGH 3 minutes.
3. Combine sugar and coffee mixtures. Cool completely.
4. Add vodka, vanilla bean and glycerin to sugar/coffee mixture. Mix well and pour into 2 empty liqueur bottles, cap and store at least 2 weeks before serving.

* Glycerin is used to obtain a smoother liqueur and can be purchased in most drug stores.

Hot Chocolate Mix

3⅓ cups	skim milk powder	825 mL
¼ cup	icing sugar	50 mL
½ cup	Nestlé's Quik	125 mL
⅓ cup	Coffee Mate	75 mL

1. Mix ingredients together in a 4-cup (1 L) airtight container.
2. Add 1 tbsp. (15 mL) of mix to 1 cup (250 mL) boiling water. Stir and enjoy.

Low-Cal Hot Chocolate

3 cups	skim milk powder	750 mL
¾ cup	cocoa (unsweetened)	175 mL
⅓ cup	sugar sweetener (Sweet n' Low)*	75 mL

1. Combine above ingredients and place in blender. Blend until well combined. Store in airtight container.
2. Add 2 heaping tbsp. (30 + mL) of cocoa per 1 cup (250 mL) boiling water. Stir and enjoy.

*   Add more sugar substitute to taste.

15

Hot Buttered Rum

2	whole cloves	2
2	whole allspice	2
1	stick cinnamon	1
1	tsp. sugar	5 mL
	water	
2 oz.	amber rum	50 mL
	boiling water	
1 tsp.	unsalted butter	5 mL

1. Place spices and sugar in a large coffee mug. Add 1-2 tbsp. water. Microwave on HIGH 20-30 seconds or until boiling. Let stand 5 minutes.
2. In a custard cup, heat rum for 20 seconds on HIGH and add to spice mixture, stir and fill to top with boiling water. Add butter, stir and serve.

 40

Hot Egg Nog

¾ cup	milk	175 mL
1	egg	1
1 tbsp.	sugar	15 mL
pinch	salt	pinch
2 oz.	brandy	50 mL
1 tsp.	rum	5 mL
dash	nutmeg	dash
dash	cinnamon	dash
	whipped cream, optional	

1. Microwave milk in a 4-cup (1 L) measure for 1½ minutes on HIGH. Do not boil.
2. In separate bowl, beat egg, sugar and salt until thick and lemon-colored. Add brandy and rum.
3. Slowly whisk egg mixture into hot milk. Pour into a large coffee mug. Sprinkle with a dash of nutmeg and cinnamon and top with a dollop of whipped cream if desired.

Swedish Glog (Gluvein)

8-9 cups	dry red wine	2 L
1 cup	brandy	250 mL
½ cup	sugar	125 mL
16	whole cloves	16
8	2" pieces of stick cinnamon	8

1. Combine the above ingredients in large microwave-safe bowl.* Microwave on HIGH, covered, 10-14 minutes or until mixture comes to a boil.
2. Reduce power to MEDIUM, and microwave an additional 5 minutes. Strain out cinnamon and cloves. Serve piping hot.

* Do not use a good crystal bowl in the microwave as it may not be heat-proof.

Friendship Tea

½ cup	powdered orange-flavored presweetened crystals*	125 mL
½ cup	powdered lemon-flavored presweetened crystals*	125 mL
½ cup	instant tea	125 mL
1 tsp.	ground cinnamon	5 mL

1. Combine all above ingredients. Store in an airtight container.
2. Add 1 to 2 tsp. (5-10 mL) of the mix to 1 cup (250 mL) water.
3. Microwave 1½ to 2 minutes or until boiling.

* For low cal drinks use diet crystals.
  See photograph page 128.

Swiss Mocha

1 cup	powdered instant coffee	250 mL
2 cups	Nestlé's Quik	500 mL
2 cups	Coffee Mate	500 mL
½ cup	sugar	125 mL
1 tsp.	cinnamon	5 mL

1. Mix ingredients together in a 4-cup (1 L) airtight container.
2. Add 1 tbsp. (15 mL) of mix to boiling water. Stir and enjoy.

COOK

POWER
LEVEL

TIME

1	2	3
4	5	6
7	8	9

0   CLEAR

START

POWER LEVEL

MMMarvelous MMMeatballs

Grape jelly you say? Absolutely delicious!

1 lb.	ground beef	250 g
½ cup	dry bread crumbs	125 mL
1	egg	1
1 tsp.	seasoned salt	5 mL
¼ tsp.	garlic powder	1 mL
¼ tsp.	onion powder	1 mL
¼ tsp.	seasoned pepper	1 mL

1. Combine above ingredients and roll into 1" (2.5 cm) round meatballs.
2. Place in the bottom of a large casserole, cover, and microwave on HIGH for 6-8 minutes, or until meatballs just lose their pink color. Drain well.
3. Serve with Super Sauce below.

Super Sauce:*

¾ cup	grape, cherry or apple jelly	175 mL
¾ cup	chili sauce	175 mL
¼ cup	soy sauce	50 mL

1. Combine above ingredients in a 4-cup (1 L) measure and microwave, uncovered, on HIGH for 2½ minutes. Stir.
2. Pour over partially cooked meatballs and microwave, covered, on MEDIUM HIGH for 4-6 minutes, or until heated through.

* This sauce is also great with cocktail franks, diagonally-sliced wieners or ham. See photograph page 16.

Mazatlán Madness

A great crowd pleaser!

1 lb.	lean ground beef	500 g
1	medium onion, chopped	1
16 oz. can	refried beans	483 mL
4 oz. can	green chilies, drained, chopped	113 mL
½ cup	shredded Monterey Jack cheese	125 mL
¾ cup	taco sauce	175 mL
1	medium avocado, mashed	1
1	cup sour cream	250 mL
¼ cup	chopped green onion	50 mL
8 oz. can	pitted ripe olives, sliced	250 mL
8 oz. pkg.	tortilla chips	250 g

1. Microwave ground beef and onion on HIGH until browned, approximately 3 minutes. Stir and break up pieces frequently. This can be done very successfully with a wire whisk, used like a potato masher. Drain off excess fat.
2. Spread the refried beans into a shallow 9" (23 cm) round microwave dish and top with the meat mixture.
3. Layer chilies, cheese and taco sauce on top of the meat.
4. Microwave on HIGH for 5 minutes.
5. Combine the avocado and sour cream and spoon over the heated mixture. Garnish with the green onions and olives.
6. Serve with plenty of people and tortilla chips.

Serves 20. This recipe can be cut in half, but be sure to also reduce cooking time by at least one third.

Baby Corn and Ham Rollups

A quick appetizer that can be made up ahead of time and popped in the microwave just before serving.

8	slices UNPROCESSED cheese*	8
8	thin slices of cooked ham	8
14 oz.	can baby corn **	398 mL

1. Place cheese over the ham.
2. Top with baby corn and roll, securing with toothpicks.
3. Slice into thirds and refrigerate until needed.
4. Microwave 10 to 12 pieces at a time on a dinner or pie plate for 2-2½ minutes on HIGH or JUST UNTIL THE CHEESE BEGINS TO MELT. Serve immediately.

* DO NOT use processed cheese as it melts too quickly. Although Swiss cheese has a unique flavor you may use Cheddar or mozzarella cheese.

** In place of the baby corn, you could use ONE of the following: asparagus spears, green or yellow beans or thinly sliced baby gherkins or dills.
See photograph page 16.

Sumptuous Sausage-Stuffed Mushroom Caps

Although there are many recipes for stuffed mushrooms we feel this one is the best! It is also nice served with a main course.

15	large mushrooms	15
½ lb.	ground sausage meat	250 g
½ cup	cracker crumbs	125 mL
½ cup	grated Cheddar cheese	125 mL
½ cup	sour cream or unflavored yogurt	125 mL

1. Carefully remove stems from mushrooms.
2. Chop stems and place in a glass bowl with sausage meat.
3. Microwave on HIGH for 2-2½ minutes or until the meat loses its pink color.
4. Add the cracker crumbs and cheese. Mix well.
5. Slowly add the sour cream, until the mixture just holds together.
6. Place a scoop of this mixture in each mushroom cap and arrange in a circular pattern on a plate. Cool completely before reheating.* For your convenience, prepare these earlier in the day. The stuffing can be frozen and used when needed.
7. Microwave on HIGH 1½-2 minutes until the caps are fork-tender and the filling bubbly.

* If the filling is not completely cool, it will boil out of the caps. If mushrooms caps are extra large, you may want to microwave them 2-3 minutes on HIGH prior to stuffing.

See photograph page 16.

Saturday Night Snack

This very popular snack will become even more so because it is so much faster to prepare in the microwave!

¼ cup	butter	50 mL
1 tbsp.	Worcestershire sauce	15 mL
1 tsp.	garlic salt	5 mL
1 tsp.	onion salt	5 mL
1 cup	EACH, Cheerios, Life and Shreddies (or Wheat Chex) dry cereal	250 mL
½ cup	pretzel sticks	125 mL
½ cup	mixed nuts or peanuts	125 mL

23

Saturday Night Snack (cont'd)

1. In 2-cup (500 mL) measure microwave butter, Worcestershire sauce and seasonings on HIGH, uncovered, 1 minute or until completely melted. Stir.
2. Combine remaining ingredients in a large bowl and pour seasoned butter over all. Mix thoroughly.
3. Microwave, uncovered, on HIGH, 3-4 minutes, STIRRING AFTER EACH MINUTE. Mixture will be moist, but will dry and crisp after standing and cooling for approximately 10 minutes.

Yields 4 cups.
For double the amount above, microwave 6-8 minutes.

Teriyaki Chicken

Finger licking good!

1 cup	soy sauce	250 mL
½ cup	sherry	125 mL
½ cup	sugar	125 mL
1	onion, finely chopped	1
2	cloves garlic, minced	2
2 tsp.	powdered ginger	10 mL
1 lb.	chicken wings (tips removed and cut at the joint)	500 g

1. Mix all the above, except chicken.
2. Pour marinade* over chicken and let stand 4-6 hours. Do not marinate any longer than 12 hours, or chicken will darken unattractively.
3. Place chicken in a circular pattern on a platter with thicker ends pointing towards the outside.
4. Cover with wax paper.
5. Microwave on HIGH for 7-8 minutes. Let stand 5-10 minutes. Check one piece of chicken. It should no longer be pink inside. Microwave additional time if needed.

* This marinade can be made ahead of time and stored in the refrigerator. It is great with pork, or for a nice change, substitute with round steak cut into strips. Marinade can be reused. If you wish to serve a thick sauce with the chicken, add 2 tbsp. (25 mL) cornstarch to the marinade, and microwave on HIGH 2-3 minutes, stirring occasionally, or until the mixture is thickened.

Hot and Pleasin' Mushroom Dip

½ lb.	fresh mushrooms, finely chopped	250 g
½ cup	finely chopped green onion	125 mL
¼ cup	butter	50 mL
2 tbsp.	flour	25 mL
1 cup	sour cream, divided	250 mL
¼ cup	milk	50 mL
½ tsp.	EACH salt, pepper, paprika & dry hot mustard	2 mL
dash	Tabasco sauce	1 mL
dash	Worcestershire sauce	1 mL

1. Microwave mushrooms and onions in butter on HIGH for 2-3 minutes, or until onions are tender.
2. Sprinkle with flour and stir until smooth.
3. Mix in ½ cup (125 mL) of the sour cream, and milk.
4. Microwave on HIGH for 3 minutes or until mixture thickens, stirring every ½ minute.
5. Stir in the other ½ cup (125 mL) of sour cream and the remaining seasonings. Serve hot with crackers on the side. Excellent as a vegetable dip.

California Crab Dip

This one is a breeze and boy is it good!

14 oz. can	artichoke hearts, finely chopped	398 mL
½ cup	grated Parmesan cheese	125 mL
½ cup	mayonnaise	125 mL
½ cup	sour cream	125 mL
½ tsp.	garlic salt	2 mL
1 tsp.	lemon juice	5 mL
dash	Worcestershire sauce	1 mL
4 oz. can	crab or shrimp, drained	113 g

1. Combine the above ingredients in a 1-quart (1 L) bowl.
2. Microwave on HIGH for 2-3 minutes or until warmed through.
3. Serve with assorted crackers and friends.

For a variation of the above, combine all of the ingredients EXCEPT crab and pour over a bed of crab on the half shell. It is also excellent served over a bed of hot, fluffy, white rice.

See photograph page 16.

25

Zing Zang Dip

This hot dip is a sure hit with those who like a zing to their food.

1	small onion, finely chopped	1	
2 tbsp.	butter	25	mL
1 cup	chopped and drained, canned tomatoes	250	mL
6 oz. can	pickled green chilies, chopped	170	g
1 tsp.	sweet basil	5	mL
½ tsp.	salt	2	mL
¼ tsp.	pepper	1	mL
½ lb.	Monterey Jack cheese, shredded	250	g
1 cup	cream	250	mL

1. Microwave onions in butter for 2 minutes on HIGH or until onions are transparent.
2. Add tomatoes, chilies, basil, salt and pepper, and microwave on MEDIUM 10 minutes to blend flavours!
3. Add cheese and cream and microwave another 2 minutes on MEDIUM, stirring every minute. DO NOT BOIL, or dip will curdle. Serve hot with nacho or taco chips or an assortment of raw vegetables.

Cheese Bread

1 loaf	French bread at room temperature	1	loaf
1 cup	soft butter	250	mL
1½ tsp.	poppy seeds, plus extra for sprinkling	7	mL
2 tbsp.	finely chopped green onion	25	mL
¾ tsp.	dry or Dijon mustard	4	mL
8 slices	Swiss cheese, processed or otherwise, cut diagonally	8	

1. Slice the French loaf at an angle into 16ths, NOT cutting through to the bottom.
2. Combine butter, poppy seeds, onion and mustard.
3. Spread some butter between slices and remaining butter all over the loaf.
4. Insert cheese slices, TIPS POINTED UPWARD.
5. Sprinkle the top of the loaf with additional poppy seeds.
6. Place on a dinner plate, cover with waxed paper and microwave on HIGH 50 to 60 seconds or until the cheese has melted.
   See photograph page 48.

COOK

POWER
LEVEL

TIME

1	2	3
4	5	6
7	8	9
0		CLEAR

START

POWER LEVEL

Buttermilk Bran Muffins

This makes a LARGE batch that will keep in the refrigerator up to 6 weeks.

2 cups	All-Bran cereal	500 mL
2 cups	boiling water	500 mL
4 cups	flour	1 L
1 cup	wheat germ	250 mL
4 cups	bran flakes	1 L
2 cups	white sugar	500 mL
3 tbsp.	baking soda	45 mL
1 tsp.	salt	5 mL
2½ cups	raisins	625 mL
4	eggs	4
4½ cups	buttermilk	1 L
1 cup	oil	250 mL

1. Combine All-Bran and boiling water. Cool.
2. In a large bowl mix flour, wheat germ, bran flakes, white sugar, baking soda, salt and raisins.
3. Add eggs, buttermilk, oil and cooled All-Bran-water mixture. Mix well with electric beater.
4. Cover and refrigerate 24 hours BEFORE USING.
5. When ready to use spoon mixture into muffin papers, no more than ½ full.
6. Microwave on HIGH, uncovered, until no longer doughy.

   Cooking Times:
   1 muffin ½-¾ minute
   2 muffins ¾-1¼ minutes
   4 muffins 1¼-1¾ minutes
   6 muffins 1¾-2¼ minutes

Orange Muffins

Delicious and very nutritious.

¾ cup	pitted dates OR raisins	175 mL
1	unpeeled orange, cut into 8 sections	1
2	eggs	2
½ cup	orange juice	125 mL
½ cup	butter or margarine	125 mL
1 cup	whole-wheat flour	250 mL
1¼ cups	all-purpose flour	300 mL
¾ cup	granulated sugar	175 mL
2 tsp.	baking soda	10 mL
1 tsp.	salt	5 mL

1. Place the first 5 ingredients in a blender and blend until smooth.
2. Sift dry ingredients together.
3. Combine wet and dry ingredients, stirring until evenly moistened. DO NOT OVER-MIX.
4. Spoon mixture into muffin papers filling no more than ½ full.
5. Microwave on HIGH 20-30 seconds per muffin or until the muffins lose their batter-like appearance on the surface.

* This recipe may be made-up ahead and stored in the refrigerator up to 6 weeks. Muffins will cook more evenly if batter is at room temperature.

Banana Health Bread

½ cup	melted margarine or butter	125 mL
½ cup	brown sugar, packed	125 mL
2	eggs, slightly beaten	2
⅓ cup	hot tap water	75 mL
1 cup	mashed ripe bananas (3 small)	250 mL
1 cup	wheat germ	250 mL
1 cup	whole-wheat flour	250 mL
1 tsp.	baking soda	5 mL
pinch	salt	1 mL
½ cup	walnuts or sunflower seeds	125 mL

Banana Health Bread (cont'd)

1. Combine butter, brown sugar, eggs, hot water, and bananas. Beat well.
2. Add remaining ingredients. Stir until smooth.
3. Pour into an 8" (20 cm), well-greased ring mold.
4. Microwave COVERED with a lid or plate on HIGH 4 minutes; UNCOVER and microwave and additional 3-4 minutes or until set. Let stand for 5-10 minutes before removing from the ring mold.

Nothin' Fancy Muffins

2 cups	sifted all-purpose flour	500 mL
⅓ cup	sugar	75 mL
3 tsp.	baking powder	15 mL
½ tsp.	salt	2 mL
1	egg, well-beaten	1
1 cup	milk	250 mL
¼ cup	butter, melted	50 mL

1. Combine and mix first 4 ingredients. Set aside.
2. Combine egg, milk and melted butter.
3. Stir wet ingredients into dry very gently, just until the dry ingredients are blended. DO NOT OVERMIX.
4. Fill paper muffin liners ½ full with batter, and place in microwave muffin pan.
5. Microwave on HIGH 20-30 seconds per muffin or until muffin surfaces JUST lose their wet appearance.

VARIATIONS FOR NOTHIN' FANCY MUFFINS

Blueberry: Add 1 cup (250 mL) of fresh blueberries. Fold in gently, after Step #3.
Strawberry: Add 1 cup (250 mL) fresh strawberries. Fold in gently, after Step #3.
Chocolate Chip: Add ¾ cup (175 mL) chocolate chips. Fold in gently, after Step #3.

Banana Bran Muffins

1¼ cups	mashed bananas (3 bananas)	300 mL
4	eggs	4
1½ cups	brown sugar	375 mL
1 cup	vegetable oil	250 mL
½ cup	buttermilk	125 mL
1½ cup	whole-wheat flour	375 mL
1½ cups	natural bran	375 mL
1 tbsp.	baking powder	15 mL
1 tsp.	baking soda	5 mL
1 tsp.	salt	5 mL

1. In mixing bowl, combine bananas and eggs, beat until smooth. Blend in sugar, oil and buttermilk.
2. In a large bowl, mix together dry ingredients.
3. Add liquid to dry ingredients, stir until moistened. Do not overmix.
4. Spoon into muffin cups, no more than half full.
5. Microwave on HIGH for 20-30 seconds per muffin or just until the muffins lose their batter-like appearance.

* The batter may be made up ahead of time and stored in the refrigerator up to 6 weeks.

Granola

7 cups	large flake oatmeal	1.75 L
1 cup	unsweetened coconut	250 mL
1 cup	wheat germ	250 mL
½ cup	shelled sunflower seeds	125 mL
½ cup	honey	125 mL
½ cup	water	125 mL
½ cup	corn oil	125 mL
½ tsp.	vanilla	2 mL
½ tsp.	salt	2 mL

Granola

1. In a large bowl, combine first 5 ingredients.
2. Gradually add remaining 4 ingredients. Mix well.
3. Divide in half and spread one half in large wide casserole or cooking tray and microwave on MEDIUM 8-12 minutes until golden brown, stirring at least once. Repeat with second half.
4. If desired, add nuts, dried fruits or chopped raisins after microwaving granola. DO NOT MICROWAVE FRUIT OR NUTS with granola mixture.

Store in a covered container and serve with milk for breakfast or eat dry as a snack. Can also be used on top of a fruit crisp (see page 138) or in our variations of Granola Bars (see page 155).

Basic Crêpes

1¼ cups	flour	300 mL
3	eggs	3
1½ cups	milk	375 mL
2 tbsp.	melted butter	25 mL
	dash of salt	

1. Place ALL of the above ingredients in a blender and blend until the consistency of thick whipping cream. You may also use an electric mixer.
2. Let the batter STAND 1 hour for perfect crêpes.
3. Pour ¼ cup of batter in a crêpe pan or a Teflon-coated fry pan. Cook over medium heat until lightly browned. Remove with spatula, stack to cool.*

* Prepare crêpes ahead of time, freeze and use when needed.
To defrost crêpes in the microwave, the following timings apply on HIGH:
2 crêpes 50-60 seconds
4 crêpes 1-1½ minutes
6 crêpes 1½-2 minutes

Cream Cheese and Shrimp Crêpes

Succulent pink shrimp combined with creamy sauce fill these savory crêpes to provide a superb beginning to an elegant dinner. Extremely Rich!

12	cooked crêpes (see page 32)	12
1 cup	cream cheese, softened	250 mL
1 cup	half-and-half, or cream	250 mL
½ tsp.	dill	2 mL
2 tbsp.	fresh lemon juice	30 mL
	salt and pepper to taste	
1 lb.	cooked shrimp*	500 g
½ cup	grated Cheddar cheese	125 mL

1. Place cream cheese, cream and seasonings in a large bowl. Microwave, uncovered, 2-3 minutes. Whisk until smooth..
2. Fold in shrimp. Place a heaping tablespoonful of filling in each crêpe. Roll. Place in a buttered baking dish.
3. Spoon remaining filling over top of crêpes and sprinkle with grated Cheddar.
4. Microwave, covered, on MEDIUM HIGH 2-3 minutes to completely melt the cheese.

* For a unique flavor use ½ lb. (250 g) shrimp and ½ lb. (250 g) crab meat.

29

Ham and Mushroom Crêpes

12	cooked crêpes (see page 32)		
1 tbsp.	butter	15	mL
1	medium onion, finely chopped	1	
1½ cups	finely chopped mushrooms	375	mL
2	medium tomatoes, peeled and chopped	2	
1 cup	diced, cooked ham	250	mL
dash	marjoram	1	mL
	salt and pepper to taste		
1¼ cups	Mornay Sauce, below	300	mL
	Parmesan cheese		

1. Melt butter, add onions and mushrooms. Microwave on HIGH, uncovered, 4-5 minutes or until onions are transparent and tender.
2. Stir in tomatoes, ham and seasonings. Microwave an additional 2-3 minutes or until heated through.
3. Divide the filling among crêpes and roll up, placing the filled crêpes in a large baking dish.
4. Pour Mornay Sauce over crêpes, sprinkle with Parmesan cheese. Broil 3-4 minutes or until cheese is lightly browned.

Mornay Sauce for Ham and Mushroom Crêpes:

2 tbsp.	butter	25	mL
2 tbsp.	flour	25	mL
½ tsp.	salt	2	mL
⅛ tsp.	pepper	1	mL
¼ tsp.	nutmeg	1	mL
1 cup	milk	250	mL
½ cup	grated Cheddar cheese	125	mL
¼ cup	Parmesan cheese	50	mL

1. Microwave butter for 1 minute on HIGH in 2-cup (500 mL) measure.
2. Whisk in flour, salt, pepper and nutmeg.
3. Gradually whisk in milk until smooth.
4. Microwave on HIGH, uncovered, 1½-2½ minutes or until mixture thickens, stirring every ½ minute.
5. Stir in cheeses, and continue stirring until smooth.

Cheesy Chicken and Broccoli Crêpes

All you need for a really super lunch or light supper!

12	cooked crêpes (see page 32)	

Cheese Filling:

½ cup	butter	125 mL
⅔ cup	flour	150 mL
2¼ cups	milk	550 mL
½ cup	shredded Swiss cheese	125 mL
¼ cup	Parmesan cheese	50 mL
4	egg yolks, beaten	4
dash	pepper	1 mL
dash	nutmeg	1 mL
2 cups	diced cooked chicken	500 mL
2 cups	chopped broccoli, cooked until tender-crisp*	500 mL

1. Melt butter in a 1-quart (1 L) casserole. Whisk in flour and milk.
2. Microwave on HIGH, uncovered, 3-4 minutes or until sauce thickens. Whisk after each minute.
3. Whisk in cheeses, egg yolks and spices.
4. Microwave on HIGH, uncovered for 1-1½ minutes or until mixture just returns to a boil.
5. Set aside ½ cup (125 mL) of thickened cheese mixture for cream sauce.
6. Divide and spoon the remaining filling evenly into each crêpe. Divide chicken and broccoli into equal portions and place on top of the cheese filling. Roll crêpes securely and place in a baking dish.

Cream Sauce:

2 tbsp.	butter	25 mL
2 tbsp.	flour	25 mL
1 cup	milk	250 mL
dash	nutmeg	1 mL
	salt and pepper to taste	
½ cup	of the above cheese filling	125 mL
¼ cup	Parmesan cheese	50 mL

6. To prepare cream sauce, melt butter in a 2 cup (500 mL) measure. Whisk in flour and milk. Microwave, uncovered, on HIGH 2-3 minutes or until thickened, stirring after each minute.
7. Add remaining ingredients, except Parmesan cheese.
8. Pour cream sauce over crêpes, sprinkle with Parmesan cheese. Cover and microwave on HIGH 4-5 minutes. Remove cover and broil 2-3 minutes or until crêpes are golden brown and bubbly.

* To tender crisp broccoli, microwave, covered, on HIGH 2-3 minutes.
See photograph page 32.

Eggs

* Remember eggs at room temperature will cook faster than eggs just taken from the refrigerator. To bring eggs to room temperature just hold them under warm running water for 30 seconds.

* Eggs cooked in wide-mouthed bowls will take longer to cook than in a narrower bowl.

Crustless Quiche Lorraine

A traditional French dish which uses up leftover vegetables or meat and adapts beautifully to the microwave.

¾ cup	chopped green onion	175 mL
10	slices bacon, cooked crisp *, crumbled	10
1 cup	grated Swiss or Cheddar cheese	250 mL
1 cup	evapo....ted milk	250 mL
5	large eggs	5
¾ tsp.	salt	4 mL
⅛ tsp.	cayenne	1 mL

1. Microwave onion on HIGH for 2 minutes in quiche dish or 8" (20 cm) pie plate.
2. Sprinkle the bacon and cheese evenly over cooked onion.
3. Scald milk in a 4-cup (1 L) measure for 2-3 minutes on HIGH.
4. Whisk eggs, salt and cayenne, add the scalded milk, continuing to whisk.
5. Pour the milk over the bacon, cheese, and onion.**
6. Microwave on MEDIUM HIGH, 5 to 8 minutes, covered. Let stand 5 minutes before serving.

* In place of bacon, use 1 cup (250 mL) diced cooked chicken, ham, fish or seafood. For vegetarian quiche replace meat with cooked vegetables.

** You could also pour this filling into a cooked pie shell. Microwave for 8-9 minutes, covered, on MEDIUM HIGH.

Mushroom Quiche Supreme

A special treat for company.

Crust:

1½ tsp.	salt	7 mL
1½ cups	grated Cheddar cheese	375 mL
1½ cups	all-purpose flour	375 mL
⅓ cup	cold butter	75 mL
¼ cup	cold lard	50 mL
4 tbsp.	iced water	45 mL

1. Stir salt and grated cheese into flour. Cut in butter and lard.
2. Sprinkle with water and mix lightly just until the mixture gathers together into a ball. Chill.
3. Roll out on a floured surface or between 2 pieces of lightly floured wax paper and cut to fit an 8" (20 cm) pie plate.
4. Microwave on HIGH 3-4 minutes. Pastry is done when it looks dry and blistered. If a golden brown crust is desired, bake at 425°F (220°C) for 5 minutes.

Filling:*

1 tbsp.	butter	15 mL
1	onion, finely chopped	1
1½ cups	mushrooms, chopped and squeezed dry	375 mL
3	eggs	3
¾ cup	sour cream	175 mL
1 cup	grated Swiss cheese	250 mL
1½ tsp.	salt	7 mL
⅛ tsp.	pepper	1 mL
1 tsp.	tarragon	5 mL
⅛ tsp.	nutmeg	1 mL
2 tbsp.	chopped fresh parsley	25 mL

1. Microwave butter, onions and mushrooms on HIGH, 3-4 minutes or until vegetables are tender. Pat with a paper towel to remove any excess moisture. Set aside.
2. Beat eggs with sour cream and stir in cheese. Add salt, pepper, tarragon and nutmeg.
3. Spread the mushroom filling over the bottom of the cooked pie shell. Top with egg/sour cream mixture. Sprinkle with parsley. Cover with a lid or dinner plate.
4. Microwave on MEDIUM HIGH for 7-8 minutes, until quiche is set but jiggles lightly in the center. Let stand 5 minutes.

* For a tasty appetizer, place filling in cooked tart shells. Microwave, uncovered, on MEDIUM HIGH approximately 30 seconds per tart.

Egg Mc-Microwave

An easy fast breakfast on the run!

1	egg	1
	salt and pepper to taste	
1 tsp.	water or milk	5 mL
1 tbsp.	grated cheese	15 mL
1	English muffin	1
1	slice of ham or bacon cooked crisp	1
	1 coffee cup, or Pyrex custard cup sprayed with Pam or coated with melted margarine.	

1. Whisk the egg and add seasonings, water and cheese.
2. Microwave on MEDIUM HIGH for 30 seconds, stir and microwave another 20-30 seconds.
3. Place the cooked egg on an English muffin, top with ham or bacon, add your favorite spread and enjoy!

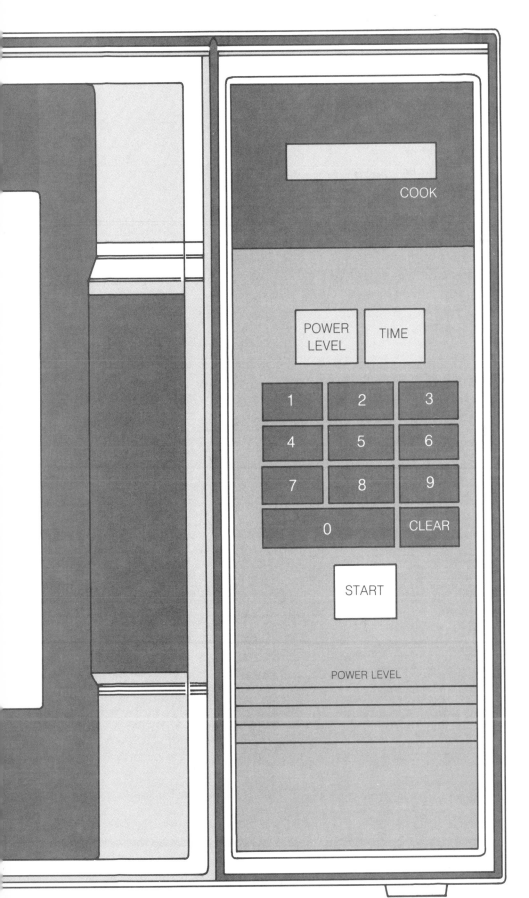

COOK

POWER
LEVEL

TIME

1	2	3
4	5	6
7	8	9
0		CLEAR

START

POWER LEVEL

Cream of Carrot/Squash Soup

An absolute favorite — nourishing too.

1	large acorn or butternut squash	1
2 cups	shredded carrots	500 mL
2 cups	chicken broth	500 mL
1	medium clove garlic, crushed	1
1 cup	cream or whole milk	250 mL
	salt and pepper to taste	
	croutons and parsley for garnish	

1. Pierce squash with a sharp knife. Microwave on HIGH for 8-9 minutes or until tender.
2. Scoop out cooked squash and combine it with all the ingredients EXCEPT croutons and parsley.
3. Microwave on HIGH 2 minutes, then on MEDIUM LOW for an additional 18-20 minutes to blend the flavors.
4. Garnish with croutons and parsley.
   See photograph page 48.

Zucchini Soup

1 lb.	zucchini (3 or 4 small) sliced	500 g
1 cup	chicken broth	250 mL
⅛ tsp.	EACH sweet basil, thyme, marjoram	1 mL
	salt and pepper to taste	
2 cups	milk	500 mL
	yogurt	
	parsley	

1. In a 3-quart (3 L) simmer pot, combine the zucchini, broth and spices. Microwave, uncovered, on HIGH for 5-8 minutes or until tender.
2. Place in the blender and blend on full speed for 10 seconds or until smooth.
3. Add milk and microwave 2-3 minutes on HIGH until the soup has warmed thoroughly. DO NOT BOIL.
4. Garnish each serving with 1 tsp. (5 mL) plain yogurt and parsley.

Tomato Bisque

This tastes even better the next day.

¼ lb.	bacon	125 g
4	large cloves garlic, minced	4
2	medium onions, chopped	2
6	celery stalks, chopped	6
2	bay leaves	2
1 tsp.	thyme	5 mL
28 oz. can	tomatoes, diced, reserve juice	796 mL
5½ oz. can	tomato paste	156 mL
2 tbsp.	butter	30 mL
3 tbsp.	flour	45 mL
4 cups	cream, at room temperature	1 L
1 tsp.	crushed cloves	5 mL
	salt and pepper	

1. Microwave bacon until crisp. Crumble and reserve bacon. Pour bacon drippings into a large bowl, add garlic, finely chopped onions, bay leaves and the thyme.
2. Microwave on HIGH for 4-5 minutes or until onion is translucent.
3. Add tomatoes, their juice, and paste. Stir well. Microwave on MEDIUM 10-15 minutes to blend flavors. Remove bay leaves. Set aside.
4. Melt butter, add flour and stir. Add cream and whisk until smooth.
5. Add cloves, salt and pepper and reserved bacon. Microwave on HIGH, 5-6 minutes stirring occasionally until mixture thickens.
6. Add to tomato mixture. Adjust seasonings. Simmer an additional 5 minutes on MEDIUM LOW.
7. Thin with milk if desired. Enjoy! Makes 8-10 large servings.

French Onion Soup

A meal in itself when served with a tossed salad.

4 tbsp.	butter or margarine	50	mL
3	medium onions, thinly sliced	3	
4 tsp.	Oxo concentrate or 4 Oxo cubes*	20	mL
3 cups	hot water**	750	mL
½ cup	dry white or red wine	125	mL
1 tbsp.	Worcestershire sauce	15	mL
	dash of pepper	1	mL
	dash of paprika	1	mL
8	half slices French Bread	8	
½ cup	shredded Swiss or mozzarella cheese	125	mL
¼ cup	Parmesan cheese	50	mL

1. Place butter and onion in a 2-3-qt. (2-3 L) casserole and cover. Microwave on HIGH 18-20 minutes or until onions are transparent and slightly browned.
2. Add Oxo, hot water, wine and seasonings.
3. Microwave, on HIGH, uncovered, for 10 minutes.***
4. Pour soup into 4 bowls, top each with 2 halves of French bread, sprinkle with Swiss or mozzarella cheese and top with Parmesan. Microwave on MEDIUM HIGH 2-3 minutes or until cheese just begins to melt.

* If you substitute with beef bouillon cube that is very salty, add 1 tbsp. (15 mL) of lemon juice to reduce the salty flavour.

** For a richer soup, add left-over beef gravy, beef stock or consommé.

*** For a full-bodied flavor, microwave on LOW for 30 minutes to 1 hour.

Caralan's Boston Clam Chowder

Served at the Boston Tea Party!

4	slices chopped bacon	4
¼ cup	chopped green onions	50 mL
½ cup	finely chopped green pepper	125 mL
2-5 oz. cans	chopped baby clams	2-142 g
3 cups	peeled and finely diced potatoes	750 mL
1 cup	thinly sliced celery	250 mL
1 cup	shredded carrot	250 mL
4 cups	light cream	1 L
½ tsp.	thyme	2 mL
1 tsp.	Worcestershire sauce	5 mL
1 tbsp.	tomato paste or ketchup	15 mL
dash	Tabasco	1 mL
	salt and pepper to taste	

1. Microwave bacon, onions and green pepper on HIGH for 3 minutes in a 3-quart (3 L) casserole or until bacon is crispy. Set aside.
2. Drain clams, reserve liquid. Add enough water to clam juice to measure 1½ cups (375 mL).
3. Add to bacon mixture. Stir in potatoes, celery and carrots. Cover and microwave on HIGH 10-12 minutes or until vegetables are tender.
4. Stir in clams and remaining ingredients. Microwave on MEDIUM HIGH for 5-6 minutes or until heated through. Do not boil or soup may curdle.
5. Adjust seasonings.

Simple Lobster Soup

10 oz. can	cream of celery soup	284 mL
5 oz. can	lobster meat	142 g
1 cup	milk	250 mL
1	onion, thinly sliced	1
2	potatoes, diced	2
	salt and pepper to taste	

1. Combine the above ingredients and microwave on MEDIUM for 20 to 30 minutes or until potatoes and onions are tender. Adjust seasonings.

Potato Soup

A substantial basic soup with good taste!

4 med.	potatoes, peeled and diced	4	
¼ cup	hot water	50	mL
2 tbsp.	butter	25	mL
1 med.	onion, diced	1	
1 cup	celery, diced	250	mL
1 tbsp.	flour	15	mL
4 cups	homogenized milk	1	L

1. Place potatoes and water in a 3-quart (3 L) casserole and microwave covered, on HIGH 6-7 minutes or until the potatoes are just about fork-tender. Set aside and keep covered, do not drain.
2. In a 2-cup (500 mL) measure, melt butter for 1 minute. Add onion and celery. Microwave 2-3 minutes on HIGH or until tender. Stir in flour.
3. Pour milk over potatoes and whisk in onion-celery mixture.
4. Cover and microwave on HIGH for 3 minutes, then on MEDIUM for an additional 10-20 minutes. The longer you simmer the better the flavor.
5. Garnish with parsley if desired.

Lickety Split Pea Soup

2 cups	dry split green peas	500	mL
1	medium carrot, finely grated	1	
1	small potato, diced	1	
1	small onion, chopped	1	
1	ham bone OR a 3" (7 cm) square of smoked ham, cubed	1	
8 cups	boiling water	2	L
1	bay leaf	1	
	salt and pepper to taste		

1. Combine all ingredients in large casserole. Cover.
2. Microwave on MEDIUM HIGH 45-55 minutes or until peas are tender. Stir every 10 minutes. Remove bay leaf.
3. Pour into serving bowls. Freezes well.

Taco Salad

1 lb.	ground beef	500 g
½ cup	finely chopped onion	125 mL
½ cup	finely chopped green pepper	125 mL
7½ oz.	can tomato sauce	213 mL
¼ cup	water	50 mL
1 pkg.	taco seasoning mix	35 g
2 cups	crushed tortilla chips	500 mL
2 cups	shredded lettuce	500 mL
½ cup	grated Cheddar cheese	125 mL
1	tomato, chopped	1
¼ cup	taco sauce	50 mL

1. In a large bowl, microwave ground beef on HIGH for 3-4 minutes, or until lightly browned.
2. Add onion and green pepper and microwave on HIGH another 3 minutes. Drain well.
3. Mix in tomato sauce, water and seasoning mix. Microwave on MEDIUM HIGH 10-15 minutes.
4. Place a layer of lightly crushed tortilla chips in the bottom of a salad bowl.
5. Layer the lettuce on top and top with the meat mixture. Sprinkle with Cheddar cheese and tomato.
6. Drizzle taco sauce over all. Enjoy!

Quickie Egg Salad

3	eggs	3
1 tsp.	pickle relish	5 mL
¼ tsp.	onion powder	1 mL
2 tbsp.	mayonnaise	25 mL

1. Whisk eggs and place in bowl or casserole and microwave on MEDIUM for 1½ minutes. Stir at least once and cook until almost firm. Let stand 5 minutes to cool before mashing. DO NOT OVERCOOK
2. Mash the cooked eggs, and add the remaining ingredients.
* This is also a great way to quickly cook eggs when making potato salad.

Creamy Potato Salad

4 large	potatoes	4	
3	eggs	3	
½ cup	mayonnaise	125	mL
½ cup	sour cream	125	mL
¼ cup	oil	50	mL
1 tbsp.	sugar	15	mL
1 tbsp.	prepared mustard	15	mL
	salt and pepper to taste	1	mL
	milk		

1. Scrub potatoes, pierce and place in a 2-qt. (2 L) casserole. Cover with a heavy lid or dinner plate. Microwave on HIGH 9-10 minutes or until potatoes are just tender. Cool completely, peel and dice.
2. Microwave eggs as directed for egg salad (see page 45) mash and add to potatoes.
3. To make the dressing, combine the remaining ingredients.
4. Toss the eggs and potatoes with the dressing. If desired add a little milk to thin out the dressing. Chopped onions, cucumbers, green peppers and celery may also be added to the salad.

Hot Spinach Salad

This is lovely served with quiche. Serve while the dressing is still warm.

6	slices bacon, cooked crisp and crumbled fine (reserve drippings)	6	
1	clove garlic, crushed	1	
¼ cup	red wine vinegar	50	mL
2 tbsp.	soy sauce	30	mL
1 tbsp.	sugar	15	mL
1 cup	sliced fresh mushrooms	250	mL
1 med.	bunch fresh spinach, washed thoroughly, broken into bitesize pieces		
2	hard-cooked eggs, chopped	2	

Hot Spinach Salad (continued)

1. Combine bacon drippings, garlic, wine vinegar, and soy sauce in a 4-cup (1 L) measure and microwave on HIGH for 1½ minutes.
2. Pour over spinach. Add bacon, mushrooms and eggs. Serve immediately. See photograph page 48.

Caralan's Lettuce Salad with Sour Cream Dressing

Our husbands exclaimed, "What is that?" They were delighted when they tried it, and there are never any leftovers.

1 med.	head lettuce, shredded, OR ½ head lettuce and ½ bunch fresh spinach, shredded	1
6	strips bacon, cooked crisp and crumbled, reserve drippings	6
½ cup	sour cream	125 mL
¼ cup	vinegar	50 mL
1 tbsp.	sugar	15 mL
dash	salt	1 mL
2	eggs	2
3	green onions, thinly sliced	3

1. Combine slightly cooled bacon drippings, sour cream, vinegar, sugar, salt and eggs in 4-cup measure.
2. Microwave on HIGH 2-3 minutes until mixture slightly thickens, stirring at least once. DO NOT OVERCOOK!
3. Pour hot dressing over lettuce, toss with bacon bits and green onions. Serve while warm!
   This sauce is also delicious over sliced tomatoes.

Janelle's Mandarin Orange and Almond Salad

After your guests have tried this salad, they will be sure to ask you for a copy of the recipe.

1	head green leaf lettuce	1
3	green onions, chopped	3
10 oz.	can mandarin oranges, drained	284 mL
⅓ cup	sugar	75 mL
6 oz.	slivered almonds	170 g
2 tbsp.	butter	30 mL

Dressing:

1 tbsp.	sugar	15 mL
½ cup	salad oil	125 g
¼ cup	vinegar	50 mL
½ tsp.	salt	2 mL
½ tsp.	parsley	2 mL
	dash Tabasco	1 mL

1. Tear lettuce into bite-size pieces
2. Toss lightly with onions and oranges.
3. In small bowl combine almonds, sugar and butter.
4. Microwave on HIGH 3-4 minutes or until sugar dissolves and almonds just begin to brown.* Stir occasionally to keep almonds from cooking together. Cool.
5. Combine dressing ingredients. Microwave on HIGH for 2 minutes.
6. Sprinkle nuts and dressing on salad and toss lightly.

* Do not completely brown almonds in the microwave as they continue to brown slightly after they are removed from the microwave.
See photograph page 32.

California Pasta Salad

1 cup	sour cream	250	mL
½ cup	Italian salad dressing	125	mL
1 tsp.	salt	5	mL
¼ tsp.	seasoned salt	1	mL
dash	lemon pepper	1	mL
2 cups	macaroni, or small shell noodles, cooked and drained	500	mL
6.5 oz. can	chunk tuna, or shrimp, drained	184	g
½ lb.	bacon	250	g
2	eggs	2	
¼ cup	chopped pimiento	50	mL
1	large tomato	1	
	parsley for garnish		

1. Combine sour cream, salad dressing, salts, pepper, macaroni and tuna. Chill.
2. Microwave bacon until crisp. Set aside to cool.
3. Place each egg in a custard cup, pierce yolk and white. Microwave, covered, for 1½ minutes on MEDIUM power. Eggs should be hard-cooked. Chop.
4. Add eggs to the macaroni mixture.
5. Combine bacon, pimiento and tomato and add to the macaroni mixture. Toss lightly and turn into a salad bowl. Garnish with parsley and serve.

Bavarian Potato Salad

4	large baking potatoes	4
1 cup	thinly sliced Kielbasa sausage (remove casing)	250 mL
2 tbsp.	cider vinegar	25 mL
½ tsp.	sugar	2 mL
¼ tsp.	dry mustard	1 mL
1	clove garlic, minced	1
1 med.	onion, chopped	1
¾ cup	chopped green pepper	175 mL
⅓ cup	sliced dill pickle	75 mL
1 tbsp.	parsley	15 mL
	salt and pepper to taste	

1. Pierce potatoes with a fork and microwave on HIGH 14-15 minutes or until fork-tender. Cool slightly.
2. Peel potatoes and slice into a 3-quart (3 L) casserole. Add sliced sausage to potatoes.
3. Combine remaining ingredients and spoon over potato/sausage mixture. Toss lightly.
4. When ready to serve, cover and microwave on HIGH 4-5 minutes, or until warmed throughout.

Honey Moon Salad

"Lettuce alone"

COOK

POWER
LEVEL

TIME

1	2	3
4	5	6
7	8	9
0		CLEAR

START

POWER LEVEL

Tomato-Smothered Steak

Serve this and you'll be smothered in compliments!

¼ cup	flour	50 mL
½ tsp.	salt	2 mL
¼ tsp.	black pepper	1 mL
1½ tsp.	chili powder	7 mL
1 tsp.	celery salt	5 mL
1½ lbs.	cross rib, blade or round steak, cut in serving-size pieces	750 g
1	large onion, diced	1
¼ cup	finely chopped green pepper	50 mL
14 oz. can	tomatoes	398 mL
3 drops	Tabasco	3

1. Combine flour, salt, pepper, chili powder and celery salt in a plastic bag. Add the meat and shake to coat. Set aside.
2. Place onion, green pepper, tomatoes and Tabasco sauce in a 2-quart (2 L) casserole and microwave on HIGH 5 minutes.
3. Add meat and microwave, covered, on HIGH 5 minutes, then on MEDIUM 15-20 minutes. If the steak has not tenderized at the end of the 20 minutes, microwave on LOW for an additional 1 to 1½ hours. Serve with fluffy white rice.

Beef Casserole Supreme

2 cups	wide egg noodles*	500 mL
1 lb.	ground beef	500 g
½ cup	chopped onion	125 mL
10 oz. can	tomatoes, drained	284 mL
10 oz. can	tomato soup	284 mL
2 tsp.	salt	10 mL
1 cup	sour cream or yogurt	250 mL
3 oz. pkg.	cream cheese	75 g

Beef Casserole Supreme (cont'd)

1. Pour enough boiling water over noodles to cover. Microwave 3-4 minutes on HIGH or JUST until they are fork-tender. Let stand 5 minutes. Drain.
2. Microwave ground beef and onion 2-3 minutes, or until beef loses its pink color. Drain off excess fat.
3. Add remaining ingredients, and fold in noodles.
4. Microwave on HIGH 4 minutes, or until heated through.

* For another serving idea, omit noodles and serve over a bed of fluffy white rice.

Beef Goulash

2 cups	macaroni	500 mL
½ lb.	lean ground beef	250 g
1 tsp.	seasoning salt	5 mL
1	clove garlic, crushed	1
1 tsp.	Italian seasoning	5 mL
1 tsp.	pepper	5 mL
1	medium onion, chopped	1
1 cup	cooked peas, optional	250 mL
1 cup	drained tomatoes	250 mL
1 cup	grated Cheddar cheese	250 mL

1. Pour enough boiling water over macaroni to cover. Microwave, uncovered, on HIGH 4-5 minutes or JUST until it is fork-tender. Let stand 5 minutes. Drain and set aside.
2. Place ground beef, seasonings and onion in large casserole and microwave, uncovered, on HIGH 2-3 minutes, or until the meat is no longer pink. Mash with wire whisk. Drain off excess fat.
3. Add remaining ingredients, except cheese. Fold in the cooked macaroni. Sprinkle with Cheddar cheese.
4. Microwave, covered, for 2-3 minutes or until heated through.

Wagon Wheel Meat Loaf

Real tasty, so easy, so good!

1 lb.	lean ground beef	500	g
1	medium onion, finely chopped	1	
⅓ cup	milk	75	mL
1	egg	1	
½ cup	bread crumbs	125	mL
dash	Worcestershire sauce	1	mL
dash	soy sauce	1	mL
½ tsp.	garlic powder	2	mL
¼ cup	ketchup or chili sauce	50	mL
¼ cup	water	50	mL
⅓ cup	honey	75	mL
½ tsp.	prepared mustard	2	mL

1. Combine and mix the first 8 ingredients in a 1-quart (1 L) casserole. Pat down gently.
2. Microwave, uncovered, on MEDIUM HIGH 5 minutes.
3. In 2-cup (500 mL) measure, combine ketchup, water, honey and mustard. Mix well.
4. Carefully drain partially-cooked meat loaf.
5. Pour ketchup mixture over meat loaf and microwave on MEDIUM HIGH for an additional 2-4 minutes or until meat loaf is no longer pink.

* When cooking more than 1 lb. (500 g) of ground beef (i.e. if you were doubling the recipe) place a glass in the center of the casserole. Arrange the meat around the glass in a ring shape. This helps the meat loaf to cook more evenly.

Home-Cooked Spaghetti Sauce

Freezes well. Pleases well too!

2 lbs.	ground beef	1	kg
1	bay leaf	1	
2	medium onions, chopped	2	
1	green pepper, chopped	1	
15	medium mushrooms, sliced	15	
1	clove garlic, minced	1	
28 oz. can	tomatoes	796	mL
2 - 5½ oz.	cans tomato paste	2 - 156	mL
¼ cup	strong coffee	50	mL
2 tsp.	oregano	10	mL
2 tbsp.	basil	25	mL
2 tsp.	salt	10	mL
¼ tsp.	pepper	1	mL
¼ tsp.	cayenne	1	mL

1. Microwave beef, uncovered, on HIGH for 5-7 minutes or until it is no longer pink. Mash meat with a whisk. Drain well.
2. Add bay leaf, onion, green pepper, mushrooms and garlic.
3. Microwave 3-4 minutes on HIGH.
4. Add remaining ingredients and microwave, uncovered, on MEDIUM at least 15 minutes. The longer the better!! Freezes well.

Serve over cooked spaghetti. See page 93.

* For spaghetti and meatballs, substitute cooked meatballs from page 57 for the ground beef.

Meatballs Paprika

Zesty meatballs in a delightfully creamy and flavorful sauce. Sure to win you lots of compliments.

3 lbs.	lean ground beef	1.5	kg
1½ oz.	envelope dehydrated onion soup mix	45	g
¾ cup	fine dry bread crumbs	175	mL
⅔ cup	evaporated milk	150	mL
3 tbsp.	butter	45	mL
½ lb.	mushrooms, sliced	250	g
2½ tsp.	paprika	7	mL
½ cup	flour	125	mL
3 - 10 oz.	cans beef consommé	3-184	mL
4 cups	sour cream	1	L
	parsley for garnish		

1. Combine beef, dry onion soup mix, breadcrumbs and evaporated milk. Shape into 40 meatballs, each about the size of a golf ball.
2. Arrange in a circular pattern on a large platter. You will need to use 2 large platters. Microwave, uncovered, on HIGH 10-12 minutes each platter or until the meatballs JUST lose their pink color. Drain well and set aside.
3. Place mushrooms and butter in a large bowl. Microwave on HIGH 4-5 minutes, or until the mushrooms are tender.
4. Blend in paprika and flour. Gradually add consommé. Microwave, uncovered on HIGH 7-8 minutes or until mixture thickens. Whisk frequently.
5. Add meatballs and microwave, uncovered, on MEDIUM HIGH for 10 minutes or until mixture is bubbling.
6. Cool for 4 minutes and fold in the sour cream. Serve over patty shells, cooked egg noodles or fluffy white rice. Serves 8-10. Do not freeze with sour cream. If freezing, freeze prior to adding sour cream.

See photograph page 80.

Moist and Delicious Meatballs

Great served with fluffy white rice.

1½ lbs.	ground beef	750	g
½ cup	dry bread crumbs	125	mL
1	egg	1	
1	small potato, finely grated	1	
1	small onion, diced	1	
1 tsp.	seasoned salt	5	mL
1 tsp.	pepper	5	mL
1 tsp.	steak spice	5	mL

1. Combine above ingredients and roll into 1" (2.5 cm) round meatballs. Place in large casserole, cover and microwave on HIGH for 6-8 minutes, stirring carefully to re-distribute meatballs after 3 minutes. Drain off excess fat. Set aside.
2. Prepare Tangy Sauce, pour over meatballs*, cover and microwave an additional 2-3 minutes on MEDIUM HIGH.

Tantalizing Tangy Sauce:*

1 cup	peach or apricot jam	250	mL
8 oz. bottle	Kraft Russian Salad Dressing	250	mL
1 pkg.	dehydrated onion soup or chicken onion soup	27	g

1. Combine above ingredients and microwave, uncovered, on HIGH for 2-3 minutes or until soup is completely dissolved.
2. Add to cooked meatballs.

* Also delicious served with chicken, fish, Cornish hen, spareribs or ham.

Quick-Step Lasagne

Fastest in the West and so easy!! Read on and find out why.

½ lb.	lean ground beef	250	g
1	clove garlic, crushed	1	
1 tsp.	sweet basil	5	mL
1 tsp.	oregano	5	mL
28 oz. can	tomato sauce	796	mL
¾ cup	water	175	mL
1 tsp.	instant coffee	5	mL
1½ cups	dry cottage cheese*	375	mL
1	egg	1	
½ tsp.	pepper	2	mL
½ cup	Parmesan cheese	125	mL
8	lasagne noodles, UNCOOKED	8	
8 slices	mozzarella cheese	8	
	OR		
2 cups	grated mozzarella	500	mL

1. In a 1-quart (1 L) casserole place ground beef, garlic, sweet basil and oregano. Microwave on HIGH for 3-4 minutes or until the meat loses its pink color. Drain off excess fat.

2. Stir in tomato sauce, water and coffee. Cover, and microwave on HIGH for 3-4 minutes. Simmering the sauce an additional 20 minutes will further improve the flavor. Simmering can be done on LOW.

3. Combine cottage cheese, egg, pepper, and Parmesan cheese in a separate bowl.

4. Layer as follows in deep square casserole or large browning skillet:**
   Half of each:
   — uncooked lasagne noodles
   — meat and tomato sauce
   — mozzarella cheese
   — cottage cheese
   Repeat with second layer.

5. Cover and microwave on HIGH for 8 minutes, then on MEDIUM LOW for an additional 32-34 minutes.

6. Let stand covered for 10 minutes.

* Do not use moist cottage cheese as the lasagne will be too runny.

** A rectangular-shaped pan does not work well in the microwave. We suggest a large 5-quart (2.6 L) square casserole with rounded corners, or a large browning pan as mentioned above. Break off the corners of the noodles to fit the pan.
See photograph page 64.

Beef-Stuffed Manicotti

Easily prepared without having to precook ground beef or manicotti shells.

½ lb.	lean ground beef	250	g
1 cups	dry cottage cheese	250	mL
¾ cup	Parmesan Cheese	175	mL
1	clove garlic, crushed	1	
3 tbsp.	finely chopped onion	45	mL
1 tsp.	sweet basil	5	mL
1 tsp.	oregano	5	mL
1 tsp.	Italian seasoning	5	mL
	salt and pepper to taste		
3 cups	seasoned tomato sauce*	750	mL
13	UNCOOKED manicotti shells	13	
½ cup	Parmesan or mozzarella cheese, optional	125	mL

1. Combine all ingredients EXCEPT the tomato sauce, manicotti shells and optional cheeses. Stuff the manicotti shells with this mixture, packing tightly.
2. Place the shells in 1 layer in a large square casserole and cover with the tomato sauce. Sprinkle with an additional ½ cup (125 mL) of Parmesan cheese or shredded mozzarella cheese if desired.
3. Microwave, covered, with Saran or a loose fitting lid,** on HIGH for 10 minutes then on MEDIUM for 24-26 minutes. Let stand uncovered for at least 10 minutes.

* See page 104 for homemade tomato sauce.
** The pasta will keep its form better if covered loosely.

Cabbage Rolls

The potato and the carrot make this dish a full meal in itself!

| 1 | medium head of cabbage | |

Core cabbage, and place in a large casserole. Add ¼ cup (50 mL) water, cover with saran or the casserole lid, and microwave on HIGH 8-10 minutes. Let stand 5 minutes. If inner leaves are not cooked, microwave an additional 2-3 minutes. Let stand 5 minutes. Cool leaves quickly by running cold water over them.

Filling:

½ lb.	EACH ground pork and ground beef	250 g
1½ cups	cooked rice	375 mL
1	egg	1
½ cup	dry fine bread crumbs	125 mL
1	small onion, diced	1
1	small potato, shredded	1
1	small carrot, shredded	1
1 tsp.	garlic powder	5 mL
	salt and pepper to taste	

1. Combine above ingredients and spoon approximately 2 tbsp. (30 mL) into each cabbage leaf.
2. Place rolls in the bottom of a large casserole, microwave, covered, on HIGH 5 minutes, then 25 to 30 minutes on MEDIUM.

Sauce:

2⅓ cups	canned tomatoes, chopped	575 mL
10 oz. can	tomato juice	284 mL

3. AFTER cabbage rolls have cooked, pour tomatoes and tomato juice over top. Reheat 5-7 minutes, covered on HIGH, or until piping hot.

Easy Out Cabbage Rolls

For those extra busy days everybody has!!

1½ lb.	ground beef	750 g
2	medium onions, finely chopped	2
1	clove garlic, minced	1
	salt and pepper to taste	
2 cups	tomato sauce	500 mL
½ cup	rice	125 mL
1 cup	water	250 mL
4 cups	shredded cabbage	1 L

1. Microwave meat, onion and garlic, uncovered, on HIGH 6-8 minutes. Stir meat frequently, or mash it with a whisk. Drain off excess fat and season to taste.
2. Add tomato sauce. Microwave on HIGH 2½ to 3 minutes, or until mixture begins to boil.
3. In a 2-quart (2 L) casserole combine rice and water, cover, and microwave on HIGH 15 minutes. Rice will be partially cooked.
4. Place half of cabbage in a greased casserole dish. Layer with half of rice, and half of meat mixture. Repeat with the second layer.
5. Microwave, covered, on MEDIUM HIGH for 12-14 minutes or until cabbage feels fork-tender.

Veal Parmigiana

1 tbsp.	vegetable or olive oil	15 mL
¼ cup	chopped onions	50 mL
¼ tsp.	sweet basil	1 mL
1 tsp.	garlic powder	5 mL
10 oz. can	tomato sauce	284 mL
4	veal cutlets	4
1	egg, beaten	1
⅓ cup	finely crushed cornflake crumbs	75 mL
4	slices of ham	4
¾ cup	shredded mozzarella	175 mL
	Parmesan cheese	

1. In a 4-cup (1 L) measure combine oil and onions. Microwave on HIGH 3 minutes.
2. Add seasonings and tomato sauce. Microwave on HIGH 2-3 minutes until sauce is hot and somewhat thickened. Set aside.
3. Dip veal in beaten egg, then in cornflake crumbs. Place veal in a large baking dish.
4. Cover with wax paper and microwave on MEDIUM 3½ to 5 minutes or until the veal is fork-tender, and is just loosing its pink color.
5. Top with ham, cheese, and tomato sauce. Cover with Parmesan cheese.
6. Microwave on MEDIUM for 2-3 minutes or until cheese melts.
   See photograph page 64.

Corned Beef

This takes a week to cure, but is well worth the wait!

3 qts.	boiling water	3	L
⅔ cup	brown sugar	150	mL
1 tsp.	saltpeter*	5	mL
2 tbsp.	pickling spice	25	mL
4-5 lb.	rump roast	2-2.5	kg

1. Combine all ingredients EXCEPT roast in large casserole, cover, and microwave on HIGH until mixture boils. Boil 1 minute.
2. Pour brine over roast. Cover and store in a cold, dark place for 7 days.
3. Remove roast from brine, and wash it thoroughly.
4. Place the roast in large casserole or microwave pot, and pour enough fresh boiling water over top to completely cover the roast.
5. Insert meat probe, set temperature to 160°F (80°C) and power level to MEDIUM. Microwave until internal temperature reaches 160°F (80°C). Rearrange or turn roast over frequently in the pot. (Total cooking time is approximately 1½-2 hours on LOW, if you do not have a probe.). Serve with boiled cabbage or Bavarian Potato Salad, page 50.

*   Saltpeter is used to help retain the pink color of the meat. Saltpeter can be purchased in most drug stores.

Thrifty Wiener Casserole

An economical meal that kids love.

1 lb.	wieners each sliced diagonally*	500 g
1	medium onion, thinly sliced	1
1 cup	hot water or enough to just cover the wieners	250 mL
10 oz. can	tomato soup, undiluted**	284 mL
1 cup	grated Cheddar cheese	250 mL
3	large potatoes, cooked and mashed or whipped	3
	dry parsley and paprika for garnish	

1. Place wieners, onions and water in casserole. Cover and microwave on HIGH for 3-4 minutes.
2. Drain water, add soup, stir well. Sprinkle with cheese. Top with mashed potatoes. Garnish with dry parsley, paprika, or extra cheese if desired.
3. Cover and microwave on HIGH 3-4 minutes until the cheese has completely melted and the casserole is warmed through.

* A good substitute for the wieners is cooked sausage links. 1 lb. (.5 kg) of sausage meat will completely cook in 7-8 minutes on MEDIUM HIGH.

** Out of tomato soup? Use seasoned tomato sauce. See page 104.

Chicken Cacciatore

2 lb.	roasting chicken, cut up	1 kg
1	small clove garlic, minced	1
1 cup	chopped celery	250 mL
1 cup	finely chopped green pepper	250 mL
1 cup	sliced mushrooms	250 mL
5½ oz. can	tomato paste	156 mL
19 oz. can	tomatoes	540 mL
2 tsp.	oregano	10 mL
1 tsp.	basil	5 mL
	salt and pepper to taste	

1. Wash chicken pieces and pat dry. In a large deep casserole mix oil, garlic, onion, celery, green pepper and mushrooms. Microwave, uncovered, on HIGH for 4-5 minutes or until vegetables are fork-tender.
2. Add tomato paste, canned tomatoes and spices. Mix well. Add enough boiling water to make a thin sauce.
3. Add chicken to sauce, cover, and microwave on MEDIUM for 30-40 minutes or until chicken is tender and no longer pink. Serve with spaghetti and top with Parmesan cheese.

Chicken and Noodles

Fast and delicious.

My Uncle used to make great potfuls of homemade noodles and chicken when I was young. These have always been a family favorite and now can be made quickly and easily in the microwave.

3-4 lb.	roasting chicken, cut-up	1.5-2	kg
2	chicken bouillon cubes	2	
2 cups	boiling water	500	mL
2 tbsp.	butter	30	mL
2 tsp.	parsley	10	mL
4 cups	wide egg noodles, uncooked	1	L

1. Wash chicken thoroughly and place it breast side down in a large casserole. Cover and microwave on HIGH 18-20 minutes.
2. Remove chicken from the broth* and set aside. Add bouillon cubes, boiling water, butter and parsley to broth. Whisk until well blended.
3. Microwave on HIGH 3-4 minutes or until boiling. Stir until bouillon cubes are completely dissolved.
4. Add noodles to boiling broth and microwave on HIGH, uncovered for 4-5 minutes.** Let stand 1-2 minutes and test for doneness. Noodles should be fork-tender.
5. Mix cooked noodles with chicken.
6. Cover and microwave 2-3 minutes on HIGH or until heated through.

* Remove skin from chicken and separate the meat from the bones if desired.

** Be sure you have enough chicken broth to just cover the noodles. If not, add more water. For a richer broth add more bouillon cubes or chicken-in-a-mug.

Seafood-Stuffed Chicken Breasts

These will melt in your mouth — a real company special.

3	chicken breasts, halved, deboned and skinned	3

Stuffing:

3 tbsp.	butter	45 mL
½ cup	chopped green onion	125 mL
½ cup	chopped celery	125 mL
3 tbsp.	dry white wine	45 mL
½ cup	seasoned stuffing mix	125 mL
5 oz. can	crab meat, or shrimp	142 g
	paprika	

1. Place chicken in a plastic bread bag, or between layers of wax paper. Flatten breasts until they are about ¼" (1 cm) thick.
2. Place butter in casserole, microwave for 30 seconds. Add onion and celery, microwave, uncovered, 2 minutes on HIGH, or until the vegetables are tender.
3. Add wine, stuffing and crab. Mix well.
4. Divide the mixture into 6 portions, 1 portion for each breast.
5. Place 1 portion of stuffing on each breast, roll up and wrap tightly in Saran wrap. Refrigerate 1-2 hours.*
6. Sprinkle paprika on chicken breasts. Place in a casserole or pie plate and microwave, uncovered on MEDIUM HIGH for 10 minutes, or until chicken is no longer pink.

Sauce:

3 tbsp.	butter or margarine	45 mL
3 tbsp.	flour	45 mL
2 cups	light cream	500 mL
⅓ cup	grated Swiss cheese	75 mL
⅓ cup	dry white wine	75 mL
	paprika	

1. Melt butter. Whisk in flour. Whisk in the cream.
2. Microwave on HIGH 2-2½ minutes or until sauce thickens. Stir every 30 seconds.
3. Add wine and grated cheese, stir to blend.
4. Pour over the chicken breasts and garnish with paprika.**

* Wrapping and then placing the chicken in the refrigerator helps to secure the rolls more tightly. If you do not have time for this, moisten the seams with water and sprinkle lightly with flour to secure the roll.

** You could reserve some of the sauce and serve it in a separate bowl.

Tasty Tarragon Chicken

Your company will be sure you've worked all day (but you haven't)!

4	whole chicken breasts, boned	4	
1 tbsp.	butter	15	mL
3	green onions, finely chopped	3	
1	clove garlic, minced	1	
2	carrots, peeled and thinly sliced	2	
¼ cup	brandy	50	mL
1 cup	white wine	250	mL
2 tsp.	tarragon	10	mL
1 tsp.	salt	5	mL
dash	pepper	1	mL
1 cup	cream	250	mL
1	egg yolk	1	
1 tbsp.	flour	15	mL
¼ lb.	mushrooms, thinly sliced	125	g
1 tbsp.	butter	15	mL

1. Place chicken breasts and butter in large casserole. Microwave on HIGH for 5 minutes.
2. Remove chicken and add onions, garlic and carrots to chicken drippings.
3. Microwave on HIGH for 2 minutes or until onions are transparent.
4. Return chicken to casserole, add brandy, wine, tarragon, salt and pepper. Cover and microwave on LOW for 30 minutes.
5. Remove chicken and place on a serving platter.
6. Strain drippings and return clear broth to the casserole dish.
7. In a small bowl whisk cream, egg yolk and flour. Stir into drippings, and microwave on HIGH 1-2 minutes or until sauce just begins to boil.*
8. Microwave mushrooms in butter on HIGH for 2 minutes. Spoon sauce over chicken and garnish with sautéed mushrooms.

* Whisk in additional milk or cream if the sauce seems too thick.

Chicken Casserole for Company

May we suggest you serve this with buttered noodles and Janelle's Mandarin Salad. See index for recipes!

3 lb.	frying chicken, cut up	1.5	kg
¼ tsp.	pepper	1	mL
½ lb.	fresh broccoli, cut into small bite-size pieces	250	g
10 oz. can	cream of chicken soup	284	mL
½ cup	mayonnaise	125	mL
1 tsp.	curry powder	5	mL
1 tsp.	lemon juice	5	mL
1 cup	grated Cheddar cheese	250	mL

1. Place chicken pieces in casserole, cover, and microwave, on HIGH 15-20 minutes. Remove the chicken from the casserole dish. Drain off excess broth. Freeze broth for use in soups etc. Cut chicken into bite-size pieces. Discard skin and bones.
2. Place broccoli in the casserole, cover, and microwave on HIGH for 3 minutes.
3. Add chicken to broccoli.
4. Combine remaining ingredients EXCEPT cheese and pour over chicken.
5. Sprinkle with cheese, cover, and microwave on HIGH 4-5 minutes, or until cheese melts and casserole is heated through.

Chicken Chop Suey

"Cabbage!" you say. Try it, you'll like it!

1	medium onion, thinly sliced	1	
1 cup	thinly sliced celery	250	mL
2 cups	shredded cabbage	500	mL
2 tbsp.	oil	30	mL
¼ cup	soy sauce	50	mL
1 cup	chicken broth	250	mL
2 tbsp.	flour	25	mL
2 cups	chopped, cooked chicken or beef	500	mL

Chicken Chop Suey (cont'd)

1. Microwave onion, celery, cabbage and oil 3-5 minutes on HIGH or until tender.
2. In 4-cup (1 L) measure whisk soy sauce, chicken broth and flour. Microwave on HIGH 2-3 minutes or until mixture is thickened, and clear.
3. Combine chicken, cooked vegetables and sauce. Stir well. Cover and microwave 2-3 minutes or until heated through.

   Serve with fluffy white rice.

Chicken In A Hurry

A real snap — with excellent results!

3-4 lb.	chicken, cut up	1.5-2 kg

Sauce:*

1	envelope dry onion soup mix	45 g
½ cup	ketchup	125 mL
½ cup	brown sugar	125 mL
⅓ cup	broth from cooked chicken	75 mL

1. Arrange larger pieces of chicken to the outside and smaller pieces in the center of large casserole.
2. Microwave, covered, on HIGH 10-12 minutes. Drain off excess broth and reserve for sauce.
3. Combine sauce ingredients and pour over chicken.
4. Microwave on MEDIUM 10-12 minutes, basting frequently with the sauce, OR until chicken is no longer pink. Serve with white rice.

* This sauce is excellent with ham, spareribs and sausage.

Chicken Cordon Bleu

4 tbsp.	flour	60 mL
1 tsp.	seasoned salt	5 mL
½ tsp.	thyme	2 mL
2 tbsp.	butter	25 mL
2	chicken breasts, skinned and boned	2
2 slices	Swiss cheese	2
2	thin slices of cooked ham	2
½ cup	bread crumbs	125 mL
⅔ cup	hollandaise sauce (see page 99)	150 mL

1. Preheat browning skillet for 6 minutes, or stove-top frying pan until hot.
2. In plastic shaking bag combine flour, salt and thyme. Add chicken and shake to coat.
3. Melt butter in browning skillet, or frying pan and sauté coated chicken breasts until lightly browned.
4. Microwave on HIGH for 6 minutes, turning after 3 minutes. Chicken should no longer be pink.
5. Top chicken with Swiss cheese, ham, bread crumbs, then hollandaise sauce. Microwave on HIGH for 1-2 minutes or until cheese just begins to melt. DO NOT OVERCOOK, or sauce will curdle.

Savory Ham Casserole

Terrific for leftover ham and rice.

1 tbsp.	butter	15 mL
¼ cup	finely chopped onion	50 mL
¼ cup	finely chopped green pepper	50 mL
10 oz. can	cream of celery soup	284 mL
½ cup	milk	125 mL
1 cup	shredded cheese (smoke flavored is best)	250 mL
	salt to taste	
¼ tsp.	pepper	1 mL
2 cups	diced, cooked ham	500 mL
3 cups	cooked rice	750 mL
½ cup	buttered bread crumbs	125 mL

Savory Ham Casserole (cont'd)

1. Microwave butter, onion and green pepper on HIGH for 2 minutes or until fork-tender.
2. Add soup and milk, stir until smooth.
3. Gradually add cheese, salt and pepper.
4. Microwave on HIGH for 2-4 minutes until cheese has just melted. Fold in ham and rice.
5. Pour into a greased 1½-quart (1.5 L) casserole. Top with crumbs.
6. Microwave on HIGH 5-7 minutes or until bubbly.

Sweet and Sour Pork

Nice served with Rice Oriental. See page 91.

2 lbs.	pork tenderloin or cubed lean pork	1 kg
1 tbsp.	vegetable oil	15 mL
19 oz. can	crushed or chunk pineapple	540 mL
½ cup	brown sugar	125 mL
4	green onions, chopped	4
1	green pepper, chopped	1
2 tbsp.	cornstarch	30 mL
½ cup	white vinegar	125 mL
2 tbsp.	soy sauce	30 mL

1. Slice meat into round pieces and pound until ⅛" (.4 cm) thick.
2. Microwave on MEDIUM for 8-10 minutes or until meat is no longer pink. Do not overcook, or pork will toughen.
3. In a 4-cup (1 L) measure combine undrained pineapple, sugar, onions and pepper.
4. Whisk cornstarch, vinegar and soy sauce in a small bowl. Stir into the pineapple mixture. Microwave on HIGH 3-5 minutes or until thickened, stirring occasionally. Spoon sauce over meat slices and serve.

Ribs in Honey Garlic Sauce

This sauce is great with chicken, meatballs or pork chops.

3 lbs.	pork ribs, cut into serving pieces	1.5 kg
	water	
¾ cup	vinegar	175 mL
½ cup	brown sugar	125 mL
½ cup	honey	125 mL
4 tbsp.	light soy sauce	60 mL
⅓ cup	beef broth	75 mL
½ cup	vinegar	125 mL
3	small cloves garlic, crushed	3
3 tbsp.	cornstarch	50 mL

1. Place ribs in large casserole, cover with water and pour vinegar over top.
2. Microwave, covered, on HIGH 5 minutes then on MEDIUM for 15-20 minutes, stirring occasionally. Drain.
3. Combine remaining ingredients in a 4-cup (1 L) measure, whisk together and microwave, uncovered, on HIGH 3-4 minutes until sauce thickens slightly.
4. Pour over ribs and microwave on MEDIUM HIGH an additional 5-7 minutes, stirring occasionally.

Nice served with Rice Oriental, page 91. Ribs are also tasty with Zesty Barbecue Sauce, page 103.

Savory Pork Chops

6	pork chops, trimmed	6
1½ oz.	envelope onion soup mix	42 g
1 cup	sour cream or yogurt	250 mL
10 oz. can	undiluted mushroom soup	284 mL

1. Place pork chops in large pie plate.
2. Sprinkle with onion soup mix.
3. In 4-cup (1 L) measure combine sour cream and undiluted soup. Pour over meat.
4. Cover with a lid and microwave on MEDIUM 12-15 minutes or until meat is no longer pink.

Serve with fluffy white rice. The sauce mixture is also great with skinned chicken breasts.

Lemon Butter Sole

The perfect recipe for fish haters!

1	green onion, chopped	1	
¼ cup	butter	50	mL
2 tbsp.	flour	30	mL
2 tbsp.	lemon juice	30	mL
¼ cup	dry white wine	50	mL
1 lb.	frozen sole, or other fish available, thawed	500	g
dash	paprika, and lemon pepper	1	mL
	finely chopped parsley		
	lemon to garnish		

1. Microwave onion and butter on HIGH for 1 minute in 9" (22 cm) pie plate.
2. Add flour and mix thoroughly. Stir in lemon juice and wine.
3. Dip the fish in flour mixture, coating each piece evenly.
4. Sprinkle the coated fish with the paprika and lemon pepper; cover tightly.
5. Microwave on HIGH for 6-8 minutes or until fish is flaky, and still slightly translucent in the centre. Let stand 2 minutes.
6. Sprinkle with parsley and garnish with lemon slices.

Rolled Sole Fillets

8	strips bacon	8	
1 cup	cracker crumbs	250	mL
1 tbsp.	melted butter	15	mL
1 tbsp.	French dressing	15	mL
1 tbsp.	chopped parsley	15	mL
3 tbsp.	water	45	mL
dash	salt and pepper	dash	
1 lb.	sole fillets, boned	500	g
¼ cup	white wine	50	mL

Rolled Sole Fillets (cont'd)

1. Microwave bacon on HIGH for 4-6 minutes or until it is just starting to crisp.
2. Combine cracker crumbs, butter, dressing and parsley. Moisten with water so that stuffing holds together. Season with salt and pepper.
3. Spoon equal amounts of stuffing on each fillet, roll up tightly. Wrap a piece of partially cooked bacon around each roll and secure with a toothpick.
4. Place fillet rolls in a large pie plate. Sprinkle with white wine. Cover, and microwave on HIGH for 5-8 minutes or until fish is flaky and opaque. Let stand 2 minutes.

Seafood Thermidor

Exquisite! A must for your next dinner party. Very easy to prepare.

¼ cup	butter	50 mL
½ cup	finely chopped onion	125 mL
¼ cup	finely chopped green pepper	50 mL
1½ cups	light cream	375 mL
2 - 10 oz.	cans Highliner Cream of Shrimp soup	2 - 284 mL
2 cups	shredded Cheddar cheese	500 mL
3	cups (approximately 1½ lbs.) cooked seafood (crab and shrimp are a nice combination)	750 mL
1 tbsp.	lemon juice	15 mL
¼ cup	sherry or dry white wine	50 mL

1. Microwave butter, onions and green pepper, uncovered, on HIGH 4-6 minutes, or until onions are tender and transparent.
2. Gradually stir in cream and undiluted soup. Microwave on MEDIUM HIGH for 7-9 minutes or until mixture just comes to a boil.
3. Stir in cheese and the seafood. Microwave, uncovered, on MEDIUM HIGH for 3-5 minutes until the cheese just begins to melt. (Mixture can be frozen at this point. When reheating, you may need to thicken with 2 tbsp. (30 mL) of cornstarch combined with ¼ cup (50 mL) of milk).
4. Just prior to serving, add lemon juice and wine. Serve over patty shells or rice. Serves 10-12 persons.
   See photograph page 80.

Bay Scallops in White Wine

½ lb.	fresh Bay scallops	250 g
2	tbsp. dry white wine	30 mL
2	tbsp. melted butter	30 mL
	lemon wedges	
	parsley	

1. Place scallops in a single layer on a dinner plate and pour the wine/butter combination over top.
2. Microwave, covered, on HIGH 2-3 minutes or until the scallops are opaque. Garnish with lemon wedges and parsley.

Coquille St. Jacques

This is a great do-ahead recipe. It can be frozen or refrigerated.

¼ cup	butter or margarine	50 mL
½ lb.	fresh mushrooms, sliced	250 g
2	green onions, chopped	2
2 tbsp.	flour	25 mL
½ tsp.	salt	2 mL
¼ tsp.	thyme	1 mL
1½ tsp.	paprika	7 mL
½ cup	dry white wine	125 mL
1 lb.	scallops, shrimp or crab	500 g
1	egg yolk	1
¼ cup	whipping cream	50 mL
2 tbsp.	grated Cheddar cheese	30 mL
½ cup	bread or cracker crumbs	125 mL

1. In 2-quart (2 L) casserole, combine butter, mushrooms and green onions. Microwave on HIGH 3-4 minutes or until onions are transparent.
2. Stir in flour, salt, thyme and paprika. Mix well.
3. Add wine and scallops.
4. Cook, covered, 5-6 minutes on HIGH stirring occasionally. Scallops will be opaque.
5. Beat egg yolk and cream together. Add to scallop mixture.
6. Spoon into 4 or 5 shells, **sprinkle with cheese and crumbs.
7. Microwave on HIGH for 2-3 minutes or until cheese bubbles.

* After the above has been refrigerated, reheat uncovered on MEDIUM for 3-4 minutes.
** If you do not have shells, use small bread-and-butter plates.

Shrimp Creole

2 tbsp.	salad oil	25 mL
2	medium onions, chopped	2
1	green pepper, chopped	1
2	cloves garlic, minced	2
2 tsp.	salt	10 mL
¼ tsp.	pepper	1 mL
¼ tsp.	rosemary	1 mL
¼ tsp.	paprika	1 mL
4 drops	Tabasco sauce	4
4 cups	stewed tomatoes	1 L
2 lbs.	raw frozen shrimp	1 kg

1. Combine oil, onion, green pepper and garlic. Microwave, uncovered, on HIGH 4-5 minutes or until tender.
2. Add seasonings, Tabasco sauce and tomatoes.
3. Microwave on MEDIUM for 10 minutes.
4. Add shrimp and continue to microwave on MEDIUM until shrimp turns pink, approximately 12-15 minutes.

Quick Seafood Curry

2 - 10 oz.	cans chicken gumbo soup, undiluted	2 - 284 mL
1 cup	light cream	250 mL
2	egg yolks	2
2 tsp.	curry powder	10 mL
4 oz. can	large shrimp	113 g
5 oz. can	lobster	142 g
5 oz. can	crab meat	142 g

1. Microwave undiluted soup on HIGH for 3-4 minutes or just until boiling.
2. In separate bowl whisk cream, egg yolks and curry powder. Add to hot soup gradually, stirring constantly.
3. Rinse shrimp under cold water, drain lobster and crab meat. Add to soup mixture.
4. Microwave on MEDIUM or until curry mixture just begins to boil, about 2-3 minutes. Serve over rice with separate bowls of minced green onion, crumbled crisp bacon, and chutney, which are to be sprinkled over the seafood curry.

Mussels in Tomato Sauce

1	medium onion, finely chopped	1	
1	clove garlic, minced	1	
1 tsp.	sweet basil	5	mL
1 tbsp.	olive oil	15	mL
28 oz. can	tomatoes	796	mL
¼ cup	white wine	50	mL
1 lb.	fresh mussels, scrubbed clean	500	g
4 cups	cooked linquini* (2 cups (500 mL) raw linquini)	1	L

1. Combine onion, garlic, sweet basil and oil in a large casserole and microwave on HIGH 2-3 minutes or until onions are tender.
2. Add tomatoes and white wine and microwave on MEDIUM 8-10 minutes.
3. Add mussels to tomato sauce and microwave 2-3 minutes or until the mussels have opened. Discard any closed mussels.
4. Pour this sauce over the cooked linquini. Enjoy.

*To cook linquini, cover competely with boiling water and microwave on HIGH 3-6 minutes or until JUST about fork-tender. Let stand covered 3-4 minutes, drain. Toss with butter, season and place on large platter.

Meeting-Night Tuna Casserole

1 cup	crushed potato chips	250	mL
1 cup	chunk tuna, drained	250	mL
4	slices processed cheese	4	
10 oz. can	cream of mushroom soup	284	mL

1. Layer HALF of EACH the above ingredients in a 1-quart (1 L) casserole. Repeat.
2. Microwave, uncovered on HIGH 9-11 minutes or until heated through.

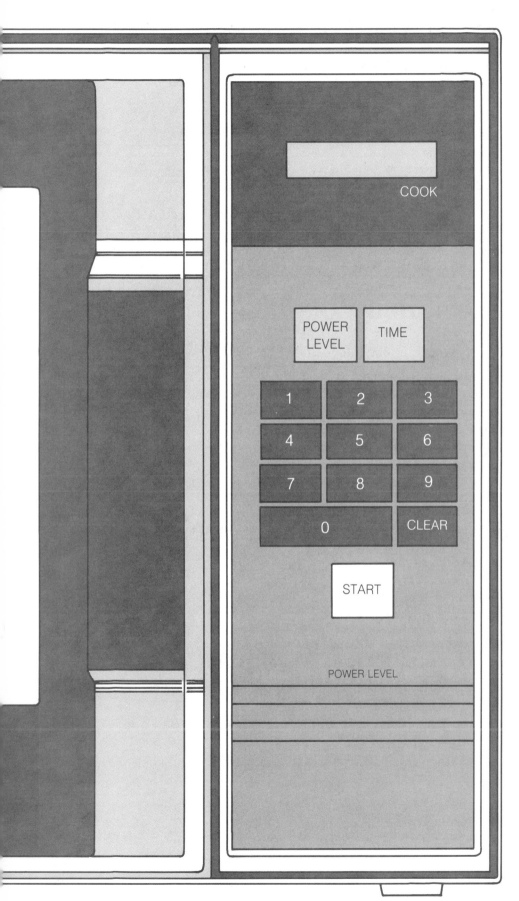

Microwaved Sweet Corn in the Husks

In the summer I pick my corn just before I cook it and what flavor. No pots of boiling water needed here!

| 6 | medium-size ears of corn, IN THEIR HUSKS | 6 |

1. Soak the corn for 15 minutes in a sinkful of cold water. Shake to remove excess moisture.
2. Stack the corn in 2 rows of 3 and microwave on HIGH 13-16 minutes or until tender. Let stand 4-5 minutes. Peel off the outer husk and enjoy.

Shrimp-Stuffed Potatoes

4	medium baking potatoes	4	
1 tbsp.	butter	15	mL
2 tbsp.	finely chopped onion	30	mL
1	clove garlic, crushed	1	
5 oz. can	drained, broken shrimp	142	g
1	egg	1	
2 tbsp.	softened butter	25	mL
⅓ cup	milk	75	mL
½ tsp.	salt	2	mL
¼ tsp.	pepper	1	mL
¼ tsp.	thyme	1	mL
¾ cups	grated Cheddar cheese	200	mL
2 tbsp.	melted butter	25	mL
1 tsp.	paprika	2	mL

1. Wash potatoes, pierce each potato 2-3 times with a fork. Microwave on HIGH for 14-16 minutes, or until fork-tender.
2. In a small bowl, combine 1 tbsp. butter, onion, garlic and shrimp. Microwave, uncovered on HIGH 3-4 minutes or until vegetables are tender.
3. Cut a thin slice from the top of each potato. Scoop out the potato and reserve shell. Whip the scooped out potatoes with the egg, softened butter, milk and seasonings. Beat until smooth and fluffy.
4. Fold in shrimp/vegetable mixture and cheese. Fill each shell with potato mixture. Drizzle with melted butter.
5. Microwave, uncovered, on HIGH 3-4 minutes until cheese is bubbly. Sprinkle with paprika.

42

Cheesy Microfries

These quick potato wedges taste a little like French fries. They're so easy you'll want to have them often.

3	medium potatoes	3
3 tbsp.	butter or margarine, melted	45 mL
¼ cup	Parmesan cheese or Kraft Grated Cheese Product	50 mL
½ tsp.	garlic salt	2 mL
½ tsp.	paprika	2 mL
½ tsp.	seasoning salt	2 mL

1. Scrub potatoes and cut them in half, horizontally, then each half into 8 equal wedges.
2. Coat wedges in butter.
3. Combine cheese, garlic salt, paprika and seasoning salt and sprinkle evenly over potatoes. Mix thoroughly.
4. Cover with paper towel and microwave on HIGH for 9-11 minutes or until fork-tender. Stir often. Sprinkle with paprika.
   See photograph page 64.

Low Cal Whipped Potatoes

3 med.	potatoes, peeled and cut into equal chunks	3
¼ cup	water	50 mL
¼ cup	Parmesan cheese	50 mL
	salt	
	seasoned pepper	
	hot tap water	
2	egg whites	2
	Parmesan, paprika and parsley to garnish	

1. Place potatoes and water in a large bowl, cover and microwave on HIGH for 8-10 minutes or until tender. Do not drain.
2. Add Parmesan cheese, a dash of salt and seasoned pepper while whipping the potatoes.
3. Add enough hot tap water to make the potatoes light and fluffy.*
4. Fold the beaten egg whites into the whipped potatoes.
5. Place potatoes in an oven-proof casserole, sprinkle with more Parmesan cheese, paprika and parsley if desired, and broil for 4-6 minutes until the top is golden.

* If the potatoes become too runny, just add more Parmesan cheese to thicken them up — it works well.

Micro Chips

These low calorie thin potato slices turn a golden brown in the microwave. Try them and see.

2	medium baking potatoes, scrubbed and thinly sliced	2
	seasoned, garlic or plain salt	

1. Spray a dinner plate with Pam. Ironstone plates work very well.
2. Place the potatoes in a circular spiral pattern ending up in the center on a dinner plate.
3. Sprinkle with salt and microwave, uncovered, on HIGH for 6 to 7 minutes, or until a light, golden brown.

   Note: The second batch takes less time as the plate will be warm. For onion and garlic flavor sprinkle onion and garlic salt, lightly, on the chips. Cook as directed above.

See photograph page 16.

Nutty Carrot Ring

Something different instead of the same ol' carrots!

2½ cups	finely grated carrots	625	mL
2 tbsp.	water	25	mL
½ cup	fine bread crumbs	125	mL
2	eggs, well beaten	2	
½ cup	milk	125	mL
1 tsp.	sugar	5	mL
½ tsp.	salt	2	mL
1 tsp.	dry onion flakes (optional)	5	mL
2 tbsp.	melted butter	30	mL
⅓ cup	finely chopped peanuts	75	mL

1. Microwave carrots and water in a covered casserole on HIGH for 5-6 minutes. Let stand 5 minutes. Drain.
2. Add the bread crumbs and mash together.
3. Combine remaining ingredients, and stir into carrot/breadcrumb mixture.
4. Pour into a greased ring mold and microwave on MEDIUM HIGH 4 to 5 minutes or until nicely set.

Baked Potato Boats

4	uniform, medium-sized potatoes	4	
¼ cup	milk	50	mL
⅓ cup	sour cream	75	mL
1 cup	grated sharp Cheddar cheese	250	mL
3	onions, finely chopped	3	
½ cup	chopped ham or chicken	125	mL
	salt and pepper to taste	125	mL

1. Scrub potatoes well, pierce each with a fork.
2. Microwave on HIGH 14 to 16 minutes or until fork-tender. LET STAND 5 minutes.
3. Cut the potatoes in half horizontally, scoop out the centers, leaving a thin unbroken shell from each potato. Hint: Use a melon scoop or grapefruit spoon.
4. Mash the potato pulp. Add milk and sour cream. Whip until light and fluffy. Stir in the remaining ingredients.
5. Lightly spoon potato mixture back into the shells, and place the potatoes in a circle on a large plate.**
6. Microwave on full power for 3 to 4 minutes.

* If your potatoes happen to become too runny from liquid you've added, just sprinkle in some Parmesan cheese to stiffen then up. It works great!

** These potatoes freeze beautifully. If you freeze 4 potatoes, microwave, uncovered on MEDIUM 5 to 6 minutes, or until heated through.

Baked Carrots and Onions

2 cups	thinly sliced carrots	500	mL
1	small onion, thinly sliced	1	
2 tbsp.	water or orange juice	30	mL
1 tsp.	Kitchen Bouquet	5	mL
1 tbsp.	brown sugar	15	mL
2 tbsp.	butter	30	mL

1. Combine all ingredients, except butter.
2. Cover and microwave on HIGH 5-7 minutes or until just fork-tender. Let stand 5 minutes, covered. Drain, add butter, stir well.

Colorful Broccoli and Carrot Curls

1	small head of broccoli	1
2	large carrots, peeled	2
3 tbsp.	water	45 mL
1 tbsp.	butter	15 mL
1 tsp.	dried mint leaves	5 mL

1. Cut broccoli into even-size pieces.
2. Peel carrots into strips with potato peeler and combine with broccoli.
3. Put water and vegetables in casserole, cover, and microwave on HIGH for 5 to 6 minutes or until the vegetables are just tender crisp. Drain if necessary.
4. Add butter and mint. Stir and serve.

May be topped with toasted, slivered almonds.
See photograph page 80.

Company Vegetable Casserole

3 cups	broccoli, cut up into small florets	750 mL
2 cups	cauliflower, cut up into small florets	500 mL
10 oz. can	cream style corn	284 mL
10 oz. can	Niblets corn	284 mL
10 oz. can	cream of mushroom soup	284 mL
2 cups	shredded Swiss cheese	500 mL
2 cups	Durkees onion rings*	500 mL

1. Place the broccoli and cauliflower in a 1-quart (1 L) casserole and microwave, covered, on HIGH for 4-5 minutes or until almost tender. Drain excess moisture.
2. In a 2-quart (2 L) casserole combine all of the remaining ingredients EXCEPT the onion rings. Mix well.
3. Fold the partially cooked broccoli and cauliflower into the corn/soup mixture.
4. Microwave, uncovered, on HIGH for 4-5 minutes or until heated through. Top with onion rings. Serve.

* Instead of onion rings used crushed potato chips, or crushed French Onion Thins.

Zucchini Combo

3 med.	zucchini, sliced	3
2 cups	sliced mushrooms	500 mL
1	clove garlic, minced	1
2 tbsp.	butter	30 mL
2 med.	tomatoes, quartered	2
¼ cup	grated Parmesan cheese*	50 mL
	salt and pepper to taste	

1. Combine zucchini, mushrooms, garlic and butter in a 1-quart (1 L) casserole.
2. Microwave on HIGH, covered, 8 to 10 minutes or until vegetables are tender.
3. Carefully stir in tomatoes, sprinkle with cheese, season with salt and pepper.
4. Microwave, UNCOVERED, 1 to 2 minutes or until tomatoes are heated through.

* For an Italian flavor add 1 tsp. (5 mL) each oregano and sweet basil or 2 tsp. (10 mL) Italian Seasonings, and mozzarella instead of Parmesan cheese.

Broccoli Ring

½ cup	mayonnaise*	125 mL
1 tbsp.	flour	15 mL
2	eggs, well-beaten	2
¼ cup	cereal cream or whole milk	50 mL
½ tsp.	salt	2 mL
½ cup	grated Cheddar or Parmesan cheese	125 mL
2 cups	cooked, chopped broccoli**	500 mL

1. Combine all of the above ingredients EXCEPT broccoli.
2. Fold broccoli into the above.
3. Place in a 1-quart (1 L) ring mold and microwave on MEDIUM HIGH 3-4 minutes or until nicely set.

* You can substitute yogurt, or sour cream for mayonnaise.
** You can substitute asparagus or cauliflower for the broccoli.

Broccoli with Lemon Butter

2 lbs.	fresh broccoli	1 kg
¼ cup	unsalted butter, softened	50 mL
1 tbsp.	Dijon mustard	15 mL
	juice of ½ lemon	

1. Trim florets from broccoli, reserving the stems for other uses.
2. Microwave broccoli, covered, 7 to 8 minutes on HIGH, or until tender crisp.
3. In a small bowl combine butter and mustard, and whisk in lemon juice.
4. Spoon lemon butter on top of broccoli at serving time.

This butter is exceptionally tasty with asparagus or artichokes and can also be used to brush on fish or chicken.

Mashed Turnip and Sweet Potato

Turnips cook just like a baked potato in the microwave. No casserole and no water! They are easy to peel and full of moisture.

1 med.	turnip	1
1 med.	sweet potato	1
2 tbsp.	butter	30 mL
2 tbsp.	brown sugar	30 mL
1 tsp.	salt	5 mL

1. Pierce each vegetable with a sharp knife in 4 places.
2. Place both vegetables in the microwave. Microwave 14-16 minutes on HIGH turning each one over after 7 minutes. Add additional time if needed. Vegetables should be just fork tender.
3. Let stand 5 minutes; peel.
4. Place the sweet potato and turnip in a large bowl and beat with a rotary beater until smooth.
5. Add remaining ingredients and beat until well combined.

Cooked carrots are also nice with the turnips.

Favorite Green Beans

14 oz. can	drained French-style green beans*	398 mL
2 tsp.	sour cream or yogurt	10 mL
1 tsp.	dry onion soup mix	5 mL
2 tbsp.	milk	30 mL
4	mushrooms, finely chopped	4

1. In a small casserole combine the above ingredients and mix well. Cover and micro-wave on MEDIUM 2-3 minutes, until hot and bubbly.

* If using fresh green beans, precook first before adding the above ingredients.

Turnip Soufflé

1	medium turnip	1
2 tbsp.	sugar	30 mL
	salt and pepper to taste	
2	eggs, separated, whites stiffly beaten	2
2 tbsp.	butter or margarine	30 mL

1. Pierce turnip and microwave, uncovered, on HIGH 9-11 minutes or until knife inserts easily. Let cool 5 minutes and peel.
2. Combine turnip, sugar, salt, pepper, egg yolks and butter. Beat with rotary beater until smooth, adding hot water if necessary, to achieve the desired consistency.
4. Fold the egg whites into the turnips.
5. Cover and microwave for 2-3 minutes on MEDIUM HIGH to reheat.

Harvard Beets

1 tbsp.	sugar	15	mL
1 tbsp.	cornstarch	15	mL
4 tbsp.	lemon juice	60	mL
2 tbsp.	oil	30	mL
¼ cup	water	50	mL
2 cups	diced, cooked beets	500	mL

1. Combine all ingredients, EXCEPT beets and microwave on HIGH 3-4 minutes or until sauce has nicely thickened. Stir after every minute.
2. Add to diced beets, stir.

   Great with pork, chicken or beef.

Beans Plus

¼ cup	chopped green pepper	50	mL
2 - 14 oz.	cans pork and beans	2 - 398	mL
1 tbsp.	instant coffee powder	15	mL
2 tbsp.	ketchup	30	mL
2 tsp.	molasses	10	mL
1 tbsp.	honey	15	mL
1 tsp.	prepared mustard	5	mL
1½ cups	crumbled bacon (about 8 slices)	375	mL
	pepper to taste		

1. In a 2-quart (2 L) casserole, combine the above ingredients, cover with paper towel or wax paper and microwave on HIGH for 5 minutes or until heated through.

Fluffy White Rice

The lemon juice keeps the rice looking snowy white.

1 cup	long grain rice, any kind	250 mL
2 cups	water	500 mL
1 tsp.	lemon juice	5 mL
	salt to taste	

1. Wash rice until water is no longer cloudy. Drain.*
2. Add water, cover and microwave on HIGH 3-4 minutes or until boiling. Microwave an additional 14-16 minutes on MEDIUM. Do not remove the lid and let stand 5 minutes. Add salt just prior to serving.

* Some package directions suggest not to wash; however, we have found that rice is lighter and fluffier when washed.
See photograph page 80.

Malaysian Rice

The curry powder and coconut give a unique flavor to this dish.

1 cup	rice	250 mL
2 cups	water	500 mL
dash	salt	dash
¼ cup	butter	50 mL
1 small	clove garlic, crushed	1
1 tsp.	curry powder	5 mL
dash	cayenne	dash
2 tbsp.	lemon juice	30 mL
¼ cup	finely shredded coconut	50 mL

1. Combine all of the above ingredients in 3-quart (3 L) casserole and microwave on HIGH 3-4 minutes. Stir to blend in the butter.
2. Microwave, covered, another 15-18 minutes on MEDIUM. Let stand 5 minutes before removing lid. Stir well before serving.

43

Rice Pilaf Almondine

1 cup	rice	250 mL
2 cups	water	500 mL
	pinch salt	
3 tbsp.	butter or margarine	45 mL
1	small onion	1
1	small clove garlic, crushed	1
½ tsp.	cinnamon	2 mL
⅛ tsp.	powdered cloves	0.5 mL
½ cup	seedless raisins	125 mL
½ cup	toasted almonds	125 mL

1. Combine the first 3 ingredients in large casserole and microwave on HIGH 3-4 minutes, then on MEDIUM for 14-16 minutes. Let stand 5 minutes BEFORE REMOVING THE LID.
2. Microwave butter, onion, garlic and spices 2-3 minutes on HIGH or until onions are transparent.
3. Mix raisins and onion/spice mixture with cooked rice, stir well and microwave, covered, 3-4 minutes on HIGH.
4. Sprinkle with toasted almonds.

Wild Rice Casserole

6 oz. pkg.	original long grain and wild rice	170 g
2½ cups	water	625 mL
½ cup	diced cooked ham	125 mL
½ cup	chopped mushrooms	125 mL
2 tbsp.	chopped green pepper	30 mL
2 tbsp.	chopped red pepper	30 mL
1	stalk celery, chopped	1
2	green onions, chopped	2
2 tbsp.	melted butter	30 mL
10 oz. can	cream of mushroom soup	284 mL
	red and green pepper circles for garnish	

Wild Rice Casserole (cont'd)

1. Mix rice, seasoning packet, and water in large casserole. Cover and microwave on MEDIUM for 20 minutes. Set aside.
2. Add ham, mushrooms, green and red pepper, celery and onions to melted butter. Microwave on HIGH for 3-4 minutes, or until vegetables are tender.
3. Combine vegetables with the soup and cooked rice. Spoon into 2-quart (1 L) casserole.
4. Microwave on HIGH 10 minutes, garnish with pepper circles.

Casserole can be prepared a day ahead and refrigerated. Bring to room temperature before reheating.

Leftovers can be used to stuff mushroom caps for a quick appetizer. Terrific for stuffed tomatoes or green peppers.

Rice Oriental

Rice is a perfect side dish for any meat or fish dish, and so easy in the microwave.

1 tsp.	butter	5 mL
1 tsp.	ginger	5 mL
½ cup	sliced green onions	125 mL
4	stalks of celery, sliced	4
10 med.	mushrooms sliced	10
4 cups	chicken stock	1 L
2 tsp.	soy sauce	10 mL
	salt and freshly ground pepper	
2 cups	long grain rice	500 mL
1	egg, beaten	1

1. In 3-quart (3 L) casserole, microwave butter, ginger, onions, celery and mushrooms on HIGH 3-4 minutes.
2. Stir in stock, soy sauce, salt, pepper, and rice. Cover.
3. Microwave on MEDIUM 20 minutes.
4. In small bowl microwave egg 1 minute on MEDIUM HIGH until set. Add to rice and stir well. Adjust seasonings and let stand 5 minutes.

For a variation add 1 cup (250 mL) chopped chicken, pork, beef or a small can of drained shrimp.

Spanish Rice

A quick meal and terrific for using up any leftover meat or poultry.

1 tbsp.	vegetable oil	15 mL
1 med.	chopped onion	1
1	clove garlic, minced	1
10	mushrooms, sliced	10
½	green pepper, chopped	½
1	stalk celery, chopped	1
1 tsp.	parsley	5 mL
1 tsp.	salt	5 mL
1 tsp.	basil	5 mL
pinch	oregano	1 mL
pinch	chili powder	1 mL
pinch	cayenne	1 mL
1 cup	long grain rice	250 mL
2 cups	chicken broth	500 mL
1 cup	drained tomatoes	250 mL
	OR	
3	fresh, peeled tomatoes	3
½ cup	shredded cheese	125 mL

1. In 2-quart (2 L) casserole microwave oil, onion, garlic, mushrooms, green peppers, celery and seasonings on HIGH for 4-5 minutes or until tender.
2. Add rice, broth and tomatoes. Microwave covered on MEDIUM for 20 minutes.
3. Sprinkle with cheese, cover and let stand 5 minutes or until cheese melts. Makes 4 large servings.

   Variation: For a full meal casserole add any one of the following: 1 cup (250 mL) of diced ham or cooked drained hamburger or 6 slices of cooked crumbled bacon after step 2 above.

Brown Rice, Bacon and Tomato Casserole

1 cup	brown rice	250 mL
2½ cups	boiling water	625 mL
4 slices	bacon	4
1 small	onion, diced	1
1 cup	stewed tomatoes	250 mL
½ cup	grated Cheddar	125 mL

1. Wash rice, add water, place in large casserole and cover.
2. Microwave on MEDIUM 18-22 minutes. Let stand, covered for 5 minutes.
3. Dice bacon and add to onion. Microwave 4-5 minutes or until crisp. Drain on paper towel.
4. Combine bacon, onion, tomatoes and cooked brown rice. Sprinkle cheese over top.
5. Microwave 2-3 minutes or until heated through.

To Successfully Cook Pasta in the Microwave:

— Use boiling water. Do not attempt to boil more than 2 cups (500 mL) of water in the microwave as the electric kettle or stove top is faster.
— Always cook pasta just until it is almost fork-tender. DO NOT OVERCOOK as the pasta will become soft. The standing time will complete the process.

Microwaving pasta takes the same amount of time as conventionally cooking pasta, however, if it boils over, the mess in the microwave is easier to clean up. The microwave is also more energy efficient.

If you are not quite ready to use the pasta pour cold water over it in order to slow down the cooking process. It can very easily be reheated in the microwave.

To reheat 1 cup (250 mL) of pasta, cover, and microwave on HIGH 30 seconds to 1 minute. For each additional cup (250 mL) of cooked pasta add an additional 20 seconds.

Macaroni

2 cups	macaroni	500 mL
3 cups	boiling water	750 mL
	pinch of salt	1 mL

1. Place the macaroni in a 2-3 quart (2-3 L) microwave pot and cover with boiling water. Add the salt and give it a quick stir.
2. Microwave uncovered, on HIGH for 4-6 minutes. Let stand 2-3 minutes. Drain.

Variations for Macaroni
Add 1 cup (250 mL) of finely grated Cheddar cheese, OR a small can of tomatoes, season with salt and pepper to taste.

Spaghetti

1 cup	spaghetti, broken in half to fully submerge under boiling water.
4 cups	or enough BOILING water to completely cover the pasta
	pinch of salt

1. Microwave, uncovered, 4-6 minutes or until the pasta is ALMOST fork-tender. Let stand 5 minutes.

If you are making a casserole with pasta, cook the pasta, let stand 5 minutes, and before you know it the pasta will be tender. DO NOT OVERCOOK. Run cold water over pasta to stop the cooking process. It can easily be reheated in the microwave.

To reheat 1 cup of spaghetti, cover, and microwave on HIGH 30 seconds to 1 minute. For each additional cup of cooked pasta add about 20 seconds.

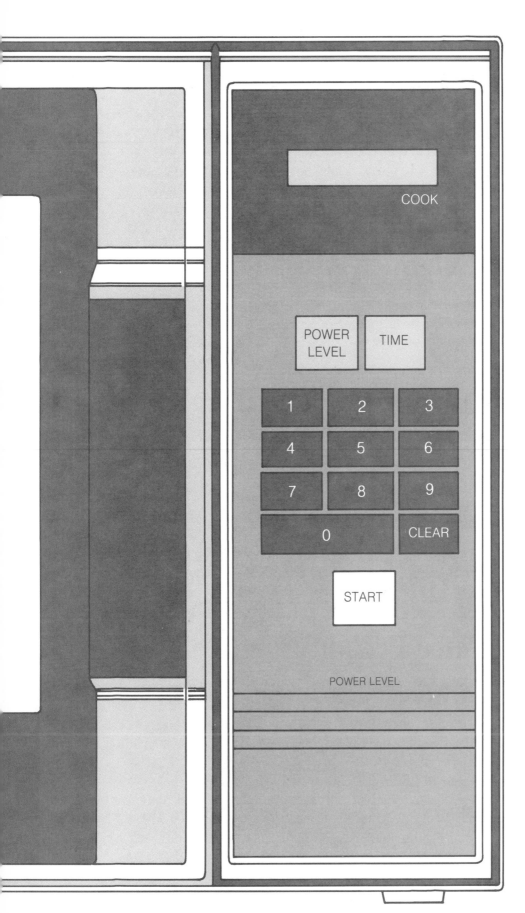

COOK

POWER LEVEL

TIME

1	2	3
4	5	6
7	8	9
0		CLEAR

START

POWER LEVEL

Sauces

Be brave! Get saucy! The microwave is ideal for sauces. No more guarding the pot on the stove or scorched bottoms! If any sauce does thicken too much, just add more liquid, whisk until smooth, and you've resurrected what could have been a disaster on the stove.

Sauce-in-a-Stick Mix

Great to have on hand!

½ cup	melted butter or margarine	125 mL
1¼ cup	skim milk powder	300 mL
½ cup	flour	125 mL
1¼ tsp.	salt	6 mL
⅛ tsp.	pepper	1 mL
3 tbsp.	water	45 mL

1. Combine butter, skim milk powder, flour, salt and pepper. Add water gradually until mixture is moistened and can be formed into a ball.
2. Roll the dough into an 8" (20 cm) rectangular slab.
3. Slice the slab into 8 equal pieces and wrap individually. Store in refrigerator until needed.

Easy Sauce Preparation

½ cup	boiling water	125 mL
1	section of Sauce-in-a-stick	1

1. Crumble sauce mix into boiled water, stir with a fork until smooth.
2. Microwave for 1 minute or until mixture boils and thickens, then add the variation (see below) that you prefer.

Cheese Sauce — Stir in ½ cup (125 mL) shredded cheese.

Tangy Mustard — Stir in ½ tsp. (2 mL) sugar and 2 tsp. (10 mL) prepared mustard.

Easy Hollandaise — Stir in ¼ cup (50 mL) mayonnaise and 1 tbsp. (15 mL) lemon juice.

Medium White Sauce

2 tbsp.	butter	25	mL
2 tbsp.	flour	25	mL
½ tsp.	salt	2	mL
⅛ tsp.	pepper	1	mL
1 cup	milk	250	mL

1. Microwave butter for 1 minute on HIGH in 2-cup (500 mL) measure.
2. Whisk in flour, salt and pepper.
3. Gradually whisk in milk until smooth.
4. Microwave on HIGH, uncovered, 1½-2½ minutes or until mixture thickens.

For a thicker sauce, follow the steps above, using 3-4 tbsp. (45-60 mL) flour and 3-4 tbsp. (45-60 mL) of butter.
For thinner sauce use 1 tbsp. (15 mL) flour and 1 tbsp. (15 mL) butter.

For Cream of Broccoli or Cream of Mushroom Soup add 1 cup (250 mL) cooked broccoli or 1 cup (250 mL) cooked mushrooms and 1 tsp. (5 mL) chicken bouillion to the medium sauce.

Quick and Easy Gravy

For every 1 cup (250 mL) of broth, whisk in 2 tbsp. (25 mL) of flour. Microwave on HIGH, uncovered, for 2 to 4 minutes. When using cornstarch to thicken gravies, only half the amount of cornstarch is required, 1 tbsp. (15 mL) to 1 cup (250 mL) of broth.

Dill Sauce

Dress up those everyday carrots!

2 tbsp.	butter	25	mL
2 tbsp.	flour	25	mL
1 cup	milk	250	mL
½ cup	sour cream or yogurt	125	mL
1½ tsp.	dill	7	mL
1 tbsp.	lemon juice	15	mL
½ tsp.	salt	2	mL

1. Microwave butter on HIGH for 1 minute in a 2-cup (500 mL) measure. Whisk in remaining ingredients.
2. Microwave, uncovered, on HIGH 3-4 minutes or until sauce has thickened, stirring after every minute.

Bordelaise Sauce

2 tbsp.	butter	25	mL
1 tbsp.	minced onion	15	mL
2 tbsp.	flour	25	mL
1 cup	beef broth*	250	mL
2 tbsp.	red wine	25	mL
1 tbsp.	lemon juice	15	mL
½ tsp.	tarragon	2	mL
1 tsp.	parsley flakes	5	mL

1. Combine butter and onion in a 4-cup (1 L) measure.
2. Microwave on HIGH 2 minutes or until onions are tender.
3. Add flour, and stir to form smooth paste.
4. Add remaining ingredients, whisking to blend.
5. Microwave on MEDIUM HIGH for 3 minutes, or until thickened, stirring after each minute.

* Bordelaise sauce is great served with roast, meatballs or steak. Add pan drippings to the sauce instead of the beef broth.

Basic Bearnaise Sauce

Excellent served over meat, poultry or fresh asparagus.

¼ cup	butter	50 mL
1 tbsp.	finely chopped green onion	15 mL
1 tsp.	tarragon	5 mL
2 tbsp.	red wine vinegar	25 mL
¼ cup	dry white wine	50 mL
2	egg yolks	2
¼ cup	water	50 mL
¼ cup	finely chopped fresh parsley	50 mL
2 tbsp.	lemon juice	25 mL
	salt to taste	

1. Combine butter, green onion and tarragon.
2. Microwave on HIGH 2-3 minutes, or until onions are tender.
3. Combine the remaining ingredients in a small bowl. Whisk until blended, then add to butter and onion mixture.
4. Microwave for 1-2 minutes on MEDIUM HIGH, or until mixture just begins to boil. Whisk until creamy.

Rich Hollandaise Sauce

1 cup	butter	250 mL
3 tbsp.	cold water	45 mL
3	egg yolks	3
1 tbsp.	lemon juice	15 mL
	pinch of dry mustard	1 mL

1. Melt butter, whisk in water, egg yolks, lemon juice and dry mustard.
2. Microwave on MEDIUM HIGH 30 seconds at a time, whisking after each interval, until the sauce slightly thickens. Do not overcook or sauce will curdle.

You may prepare your sauce to step 2 and microwave it just before you need it. If sauce does curdle, add enough milk to thin slightly and whisk until smooth.

Creamy White Wine Sauce

Excellent over chicken cordon bleu or any vegetable.

¼ cup	flour	50	mL
¼ cup	butter	50	mL
½ cup	white wine	125	mL
½ cup	chicken stock	125	mL
1 cup	cream	250	mL
1 tsp.	onion flakes or minced onion	5	mL
	pinch nutmeg	1	mL
	salt and pepper to taste		

1. Melt butter in 4-cup (1 L) measure. Stir in flour and whisk to make a smooth roux or paste.
2. Add remaining ingredients and whisk together.
3. Microwave on HIGH 3-5 minutes or until sauce thickens. Stir after each minute.

Creamy Cheddar Vegetable Sauce

Super as a sauce for cooked vegetables or try as a hot dip for fresh vegetables.

1 cup	sliced mushrooms	250	mL
2 tbsp.	melted butter	25	mL
3 tbsp.	flour	45	mL
¼ tsp.	salt	1	mL
1 cup	milk	250	mL
2 cups	grated sharp Cheddar cheese	500	mL
1 cup	sour cream	250	mL
1 tbsp.	Worcestershire sauce	15	mL
1 tsp.	dried mustard	5	mL

1. Add mushrooms to melted butter and microwave on HIGH for 1½ minutes, or until mushrooms are tender.
2. Stir in flour and salt. Gradually whisk in milk.
3. Microwave on HIGH 3 minutes, stirring every minute, or until mixture is thick and boiling.
4. Add cheese and stir until melted.
5. Fold in sour cream, and spices.

Mustard Glaze

Glaze for ham, ribs and meatballs.

½ cup	Dijon mustard	125 mL
1 tsp.	dry mustard	5 mL
⅓ cup	cider vinegar	75 mL
⅓ cup	brown sugar	75 mL
½ cup	honey	125 mL
1 tbsp.	dark oriental sesame oil	15 mL
1 tbsp.	soy sauce	15 mL

1. Combine Dijon mustard and dry mustard in 4-cup (1 L) measure.
2. Whisk in the remaining ingredients, microwave on HIGH for 3 minutes, stirring after every minute. Glaze with the above after you have partially cooked the meat.

Creamy Herb Sauce

A lovely topping for any vegetable!

⅔ cup	mayonnaise	150 mL
⅔ cup	unflavored yogurt or sour cream	150 mL
1 tsp.	prepared mustard	5 mL
2 tbsp.	cornstarch	25 mL
2 tsp.	dill	10 mL
2 tsp.	chives	10 mL
2 tsp.	parsley	10 mL

1. Whisk all of the ingredients together and microwave, uncovered, on HIGH 3-4 minutes or until slightly thickened.

Spanish Sauce For Fish

¼ cup	olive oil	50 mL
3	cloves garlic, crushed	3
1 large	onion, diced	1
1 med.	green pepper, diced	1
14 oz. can	tomatoes	398 mL
7½ oz. can	tomato sauce	213 mL
	juice from 1 lime	1
1	bay leaf	1
1 tsp.	Worcestershire sauce	5 mL
½ tsp.	oregano	2 mL
¾ tsp.	salt	4 mL
¼ cup	crumbs	50 mL
2 tbsp.	butter	30 mL

1. Combine above ingredients EXCEPT crumbs and butter.
2. Place sauce ingredients in 2-quart (2 L) casserole and microwave on HIGH 3-5 minutes or until boiling, then on MEDIUM for 20 minutes. Remove bay leaf.
3. In separate bowl melt butter, add crumbs and microwave 1-2 minutes on HIGH.
4. Pour 1 cup (250 mL) sauce over any 1 lb. (500 g) PRECOOKED fish, sprinkle with buttered crumbs, microwave on HIGH 2 minutes, or until piping hot. Serve and enjoy!

Kim's Easy Mustard Sauce

½ cup	white sugar	125 mL
1	egg	1
⅓ cup	vinegar	75 mL
2 tbsp.	prepared mustard	30 mL

1. Mix sugar and egg together well.
2. Combine vinegar with mustard.
3. Fold the 2 mixtures together and microwave, uncovered, on HIGH for 2-3 minutes or until thickened. Cool and serve with cooked ham.

Zesty Barbecue Sauce

This sauce does not require microwaving. We couldn't omit it, it's terrific! Great on ribs, chicken, leftover roast beef, ham and sausage.

1½ cups	brown sugar	375 mL
1½ cups	red wine vinegar	375 mL
1 cup	FRESHLY squeezed lemon juice	250 mL
⅓ cup	prepared mustard	75 mL
2 tbsp.	fresh ground pepper	25 mL
¼ cup	Worcestershire sauce	50 mL
½ cup	steak sauce (any kind)	125 mL
2 cups	bottled chili sauce	500 mL
24 oz.	bottle ketchup	750 mL
2 tbsp.	salad oil	30 mL
2 tbsp.	dark soy sauce	30 mL
1½ cups	beer (any kind)	375 mL

1. Combine the above and store in airtight container, or old plastic cooking oil jug. Makes 14 cups (4 L). Can be halved or quartered.

Red Currant Sauce

1 cup	red currant jelly	250 mL
¼ cup	Dubonnet wine or a dry red wine	50 mL
1 tbsp.	icing sugar or powdered sugar	15 mL
1 tsp.	cinnamon	5 mL
2 tbsp.	lemon juice	30 mL
1 tbsp.	cornstarch	15 mL

1. Whisk all of the ingredients together and microwave, uncovered, on HIGH 2½-3½ minutes or until slightly thickened.

Easy Basic Tomato Sauce

1 tbsp.	vegetable oil	15 mL
2 tsp.	sweet basil	10 mL
2 tsp.	oregano	10 mL
1 tsp.	Italian seasoning	5 mL
1	clove garlic, crushed	1
½ cup	diced onion	125 mL
14 oz. can	tomato paste	398 mL
3-14 oz.	tomato paste cans of water	1.2 L

1. Combine all ingredients EXCEPT tomato paste and water.
2. Stir well and microwave on HIGH 2-3 minutes or until onions are tender.
3. Whisk in tomato paste and water.
4. Microwave, covered, 3 minutes on HIGH and 20 minutes on MEDIUM power, stirring occasionally. The longer you simmer the sauce, the richer it becomes. Use in any recipe calling for tomato sauce.

Savory Orange Sauce

This is lovely served over duck or chicken.

⅓ cup	honey	75 mL
⅓ cup	melted butter	75 mL
1 tbsp.	soy sauce	15 mL
¼ cup	orange juice	50 mL
1 tbsp.	lemon juice	15 mL
2 tsp.	cornstarch	10 mL
¼ tsp.	salt	1 mL

1. Combine the above ingredients. Mix well, microwave on HIGH, uncovered, for 1 minute. Stir and microwave 2-4 minutes or until sauce has slightly thickened.

6   21   30

Apricot Sauce

Tasty on Cornish game hen.

1 cup	apricot jam	250 mL
2 tbsp.	honey	30 mL
1 cup	chicken broth	250 mL
½ cup	cold water	125 mL
1 tbsp.	soy sauce	15 mL
1 tsp.	dry mustard	5 mL
2 tbsp.	cornstarch	25 mL
	yellow food coloring, optional	

1. Combine the above ingredients. Mix well. Microwave on HIGH, uncovered, 1 minute. Stir well and microwave an additional 2-4 minutes or until thickened.

Chinese Honey Garlic Sauce

*This makes a great marinade as well as a sauce for ribs, chicken, fish or ham.**

4 tbsp.	brown sugar	60 mL
4 tbsp.	honey	60 mL
3 tbsp.	soy sauce	45 mL
3 tbsp.	vinegar	45 mL
3 tbsp.	beef broth	45 mL
3	small cloves garlic, crushed	3

1. Combine the above ingredients and microwave on HIGH , uncovered 2-3 minutes to blend flavors. Marinate meat for 3-4 hours prior to cooking in cooled marinade.

* To thicken sauce whisk in 1½ tbsp. (20 mL) of cornstarch.Microwave 2-3 minutes or until thickened, whisking after each minute. Thickened sauce may be poured over partially cooked meat. Complete the cooking, basting occasionally with the sauce.

Vanilla Sauce

Super served over any Christmas pudding.

½ cup	icing sugar or powdered sugar	125 mL
2 tbsp.	cornstarch	30 mL
1 cup	water	250 mL
1 cup	milk	250 mL
¼ cup	butter	50 mL
2 tsp.	vanilla	10 mL

1. Combine sugar and cornstarch, add water and milk and whisk.
2. Microwave on HIGH 2-3 minutes until thickened.
3. Stir in butter and vanilla.

Rum Sauce

Lovely over a steamed pudding.

½ cup	icing sugar or powdered sugar	125 mL
2 tbsp.	cornstarch	30 mL
1½ cups	milk	375 mL
¼ cup	butter, melted	50 mL
⅛ tsp.	nutmeg	1 mL
¼ cup	rum	50 mL

1. In 4-cup (1 L) measure combine sugar and cornstarch.
2. Whisk in milk, add butter and nutmeg.
3. Microwave on HIGH 4 to 6 minutes or until thickened, stirring every 1½ minutes.
4. Add rum and serve.

Saucy Apple Sauce

A great way to use up any bruised apples the kids won't eat.

4	large McIntosh apples, peeled, cored and chopped finely	4
2 tbsp.	lemon juice	30 mL
1 tbsp.	brown sugar	15 mL
½ tsp.	cinnamon	2 mL
¼ tsp.	allspice	1 mL
¼ tsp.	nutmeg	1 mL

1. Combine the above ingredients and microwave, covered, on HIGH 5-8 minutes or until the apples are tender.
2. Mash with potato masher for chunky apple sauce or blend in blender for a smooth sauce.

Fancy Fudge Sauce

Stays liquid when poured over ice cream.

⅔ cup	sugar	150 mL
½ cup	cocoa	125 mL
½ cup	water	125 mL
½ cup	butter	125 mL
1 tsp.	vanilla	5 mL

1. In 4-cup (1 L) measure combine sugar and cocoa, whisk in water and microwave, uncovered, on HIGH 1-2 minutes or until mixture comes to a boil.
2. Stir well. Microwave on MEDIUM, 4-5 minutes.
3. Stir in butter and vanilla.
   Yields 1⅓ cups (325 mL).

Chocolate Rum 'n' Raisin Sauce

Terrific over ice cream or any leftover cake.

½ cup	icing sugar or powdered sugar	125 mL
2 tbsp.	cocoa	30 mL
½ cup	cereal cream	125 mL
¼ cup	raisins *	50 mL
1 tbsp.	butter	15 mL
¼ cup	dark or amber rum	50 mL

1. Combine first 3 ingredients, whisk and microwave, uncovered, on HIGH 2-4 minutes or until thickened.
2. Add raisins, butter and rum. Stir until butter has melted.

* Plump raisins by rinsing them under hot tap water for 1 minute.

Marshmallow Sauce

Make your own Banana Splits and Sundaes!

4 cups	miniature marshmallows	1 L
½ cup	sugar	125 mL
1 cup	milk	250 mL
2	egg whites, stiffly beaten	2
1 tbsp.	vanilla	15 mL

1. Place marshmallows, sugar and milk into a large bowl.
2. Microwave, uncovered, on HIGH 2-3 minutes until marshmallows are completely melted. Stir frequently.
3. Pour marshmallow mixture into the beaten egg whites. Beat until creamy, 1-2 minutes. Add vanilla. Do not substitute in recipes calling for Marshmallow Cream.

Basic Chocolate Sauce

Deliciously chewy when poured over ice cream!

1 tbsp.	brown sugar	15	mL
2 cups	chocolate chips	500	mL
¼ cup	water	50	mL
¼ cup	butter	50	mL
1 tsp.	vanilla	5	mL

1. Combine the first 3 ingredients.
2. Microwave, uncovered, on HIGH 2-3 minutes, stirring after each minute.
3. Whisk in butter and vanilla. Stir until smooth.

Brandy Sauce

A lovely topping for a spice cake or Christmas pudding.

1 cup	water	250	mL
½ cup	brown sugar	125	mL
1 tbsp.	cornstarch	15	mL
1	egg, well beaten	1	
¼ cup	brandy	50	mL

1. Place water in a 4-cup (1 L) measure and microwave, uncovered, on HIGH 2 minutes or until boiling.
2. Combine sugar and cornstarch. Whisk quickly into the boiling water.
3. Add a small amount of the hot liquid to the beaten eggs and whisk. Gradually whisk the egg mixture into the hot liquid. Whisk rapidly to avoid the eggs cooking.
4. Microwave on MEDIUM HIGH, uncovered, 2-3 minutes or until slightly thickened. Whisk after each minute. Add brandy and stir until smooth.

Strawberry Sauce

Great spooned over ice cream, yogurt, cheesecake or crêpes.

2 cups	thickly sliced strawberries	500 mL
¼ cup	sugar	50 mL
½ cup	corn syrup	125 mL
2 tbsp.	lemon juice	25 mL
1 cup	thinly sliced strawberries	250 mL

1. Place thick-sliced berries in a large bowl. Crush with a potato masher or pastry blender. Add sugar and mix well.
2. Microwave, uncovered, on HIGH for 7-8 minutes. (Mixture should boil hard for 5 minutes.)
3. Add remaining ingredients. Microwave on MEDIUM for an additional 6 minutes. Stir occasionally. Cool and store in refrigerator.

Maple Nut Sauce

A delicious treat over ice cream.

1 cup	pure maple syrup	250 mL
½ cup	corn syrup	125 mL
½ cup	water	125 mL
½ cup	sugar	125 mL
1 cup	chopped pecans or walnuts	250 mL

1. Combine all the above ingredients except the nuts.
2. Microwave, uncovered on HIGH for 5-7 minutes.
3. Add nuts and microwave an additional 3-5 minutes. Cool and store in a covered jar in the refrigerator.

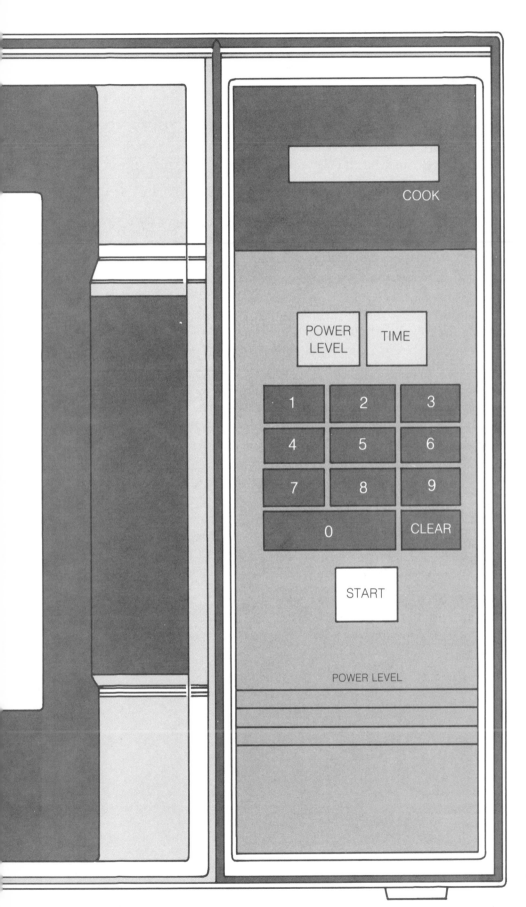

COOK

POWER LEVEL

TIME

1 2 3

4 5 6

7 8 9

0 CLEAR

START

POWER LEVEL

About Cakes

Your microwaved cake will cook differently from a conventionally cooked cake. The major difference is that a microwaved cake will not brown. Since cakes do not develop a crust, which serves to curtail expansion, a microwaved cake will have a greater volume. A microwaved cake will be moist, airy and fluffy.

Here are some helpful hints for successful cake making!

1. Prepare your recipes exactly as if you were doing them conventionally, or according to package direction. Do not change or alter quantities, UNLESS YOU ARE AT SEA LEVEL. If so decrease liquid by ¼. Cook cakes 1 layer at a time.

2. The best shape for a cake is circular. Use either a plain circular dish, straight-sided cake pan or a bundt shape. Avoid square or rectangular shapes, they do not cook evenly as microwaves cross on corners and overcook the cake in the corner areas.

3. Cakes rise higher in the microwave, so fill your pan only ½ full. Use the leftover batter for cup cakes.

4. Because cakes are more moist in the microwave, they may have a tendency to stick, depending on the cookware you're using. Greasing and flouring your pan helps the cake to release more easily; however, you may notice an undesirable coating on the cake. Lining the bottom of the pan with wax paper or any plastic wrap works well, as does spraying with one of the releasing agents on the market.

5. Cakes tend to cook last in the center. This problem is virtually eliminated by placing a casserole lid, an inverted glass pie plate or a dinner plate on top of the cake while cooking. This method helps to keep the moisture in the cake and the cake cooks more rapidly and more evenly. Most plain cakes can be cooked in 3-5 minutes when using this method. Be sure to remove lid immediately after the microwaving is completed.

6. If moist spots appear on the cake after cooking, they will evaporate during the standing time, which should only take a couple of minutes. A toothpick inserted into the center of the cake will come out clean, as it does in the conventional method, when the cake is completely cooked.

You-Name-It Pound Cake, page 117
White Chocolate Mousse with Raspberry Champagne Sauce, page 137

Moist and Rich Chocolate Layer Cake

Once you've tried this, it will be an all-time favorite! This recipe makes 3 layers.

⅔ cup	cocoa	150	mL
1 cup	very hot tap water	250	mL
⅔ cup	brown sugar	150	mL
1 tsp.	salt	5	mL

1. Microwave the above for 1½-2 minutes on HIGH and cool.

⅔ cup	butter or margarine, softened	150	mL
2 cups	brown sugar	500	mL
2	eggs well-beaten	2	
2 cups	all-purpose flour	500	mL
2 tsp.	baking soda	10	mL
1 cup	milk	250	mL
1 tsp.	vanilla	5	mL

2. Cream butter, brown sugar and eggs until fluffy.
3. Add cool boiled mixture and blend well.
4. Add flour and baking soda alternating with the milk and vanilla.
5. Pour a scant 2 cups (a scant 500 mL) of the batter into a greased and floured 9" (22 cm) round pan.* Cover and microwave on HIGH for 3 minutes, then on MEDIUM HIGH for 4-5 minutes.
6. Repeat with remaining batter. See pages 114-115 and 122-124 for suggested frostings.

* For easy removal of your cake, fully line pan with Saran Wrap. You do NOT NEED TO GREASE OR FLOUR. After each layer has cooked and cooled for 5 minutes, remove the cake with the Saran Wrap and reline the pan for the next layer.

Grand Marnier Treat

Not too sweet! A real grown-up cake!

1	Moist and Rich Chocolate Cake, in 3 layers. See page 113.	1
½ cup	Grand Marnier or orange brandy	125 mL
6 oz.	frozen orange juice concentrate	175 mL
⅔ cup	granulated sugar	150 mL
2	envelopes plain gelatin	2
2 cups	whipping cream	500 mL
½ cup	sugar	125 mL
1	thinly sliced, scored orange for garnish	1

1. Lightly sprinkle each layer of the cake with the Grand Marnier. Use only ¼ cup.
2. Combine orange juice concentrate, sugar and gelatin in a medium-size bowl and microwave on HIGH 4-5 minutes. Watch carefully as mixture boils rapidly and may boil over.
3. Stir in remaining Grand Marnier, cover with wax paper and refrigerate until completely cooled, but not set.
4. Whip cream in a metal bowl until soft peaks form, gradually beating in sugar.
5. Fold in Grand Marnier mixture. Do not overmix
6. Spread the whipped cream/Grand Marnier mixture between the layers of, and on the top and the sides of the cake. Garnish with orange slices. Chill for at least 6 hours to blend flavors.

"The" Black Forest Cake

The best! Really worth the time and effort.

1	Moist and Rich Chocolate Cake. See page 113.	1
½ cup	cherry brandy or kirsch	125 mL
2 cups	whipping cream	500 mL
2 tbsp.	icing sugar or powdered sugar	30 mL
19 oz. can	cherry pie filling*	540 mL
	maraschino cherries	
	shaved chocolate	

"The" Black Forest Cake (cont'd)

1. Sprinkle each layer of the cake with the cherry brandy.
2. Whip cream until soft peaks form, add the sugar and continue beating until stiff.
3. Spread ⅓ of the can of cherry pie filling and some of the whipped cream between each layer and spread remaining filling on top.
4. Carefully ice the entire cake with the whipped cream.
5. Decorate with cherries and shaved chocolate. You may wish to pipe some of the whip cream around the cake.

* For your own homemade fruit filling see page 146.
  See photograph on front cover.

Mocha Delight

A family favorite. Try it and find out why.

1	Moist and Rich Chocolate Cake, in 3 layers. See page 113.	1	
½ cup	chocolate chips	125	mL
2 tbsp.	hot water	30	mL
2 tsp.	instant coffee powder	10	mL
2 tsp.	granulated sugar	10	mL
2 cups	whipping cream	500	mL
	chocolate shavings, maraschino cherries for garnish		

1. Combine all of the above ingredients EXCEPT cake, whipping cream and garnishes in a medium-size bowl. Microwave on HIGH for 3 minutes, stirring twice. Cool.
2. Whip cream until it is just starting to thicken. Add cooled chocolate mixture.
3. Whip the chocolate/whip cream mixture until stiff.
4. Spread the whipped mixture between the layers and on the top and the sides of the cake. Decorate with chocolate shavings and maraschino cherries.
5. Chill at least 1 hour to blend the flavors. Overnight is best.

Poppy Seed Swirl Cake

1	Single Layer Pouch Cake Mix*	260	g
1 pkg.	vanilla instant pudding	113	g
1	small ripe banana, mashed	1	
½ cup	Crisco shortening, softened	125	mL
½ cup	water	125	mL
2	eggs	2	
2 tbsp.	poppy seeds	30	mL

Cinnamon Swirl:

¼ cup	brown sugar	50	mL
1 tsp.	cinnamon	5	mL
dash	nutmeg	1	mL

1. Combine cake mix with pudding, banana, shortening and water.
2. Beat in eggs, one at a time.
3. Beat until mixture is thick and creamy, 2-3 minutes. Stir in the poppy seeds.
4. Pour the batter into a straight sided microwave cake pan.
5. Combine the cinnamon swirl mixture and cut it into the batter in a swirling motion.
6. Cover with wax paper and microwave on MEDIUM HIGH for 3-4½ minutes. Remove wax paper, let stand 5 minutes and remove from the pan.

* Even though the cake mix may have already added pudding to the mix you still require the instant pudding mix.

Microwaved Angel Food Cake

16 oz. pkg.	Duncan Hine's Angel Food Deluxe Cake	410	g
2 tbsp.	flour	25	mL

1. Mix the cake exactly as the directions suggest, only add the 2 tbsp. (25 mL) of flour to the package marked "flour". DO NOT ADD flour to the egg white mix.
2. Pour HALF of the batter into an UNGREASED bundt pan. Cover with a dinner plate or pie plate.
3. Microwave on HIGH 2 minutes and then on MEDIUM HIGH for an additional 5-7 minutes or until the batter is cooked. Cool and remove from pan. Cake may stick.
4. Repeat with second half of the batter.

* Do not attempt to place all of the batter into the bundt pan as it will overflow. This cake is excellent in recipes calling for pieces of Angel Food Cake. See page 138 for a serving idea.

You-Name-It Pound Cake

With one simple idea, you can create the pound cake of your choice. This cake requires a 12-cup (3 L) microwave bundt pan, or two 8" (20 cm) round microwave cake pans.

3 oz. pkg.	Jell-o, flavor to match cake mix	85	g
1 cup	hot water	250	mL
19 oz.	lemon, peach, cherry, orange or strawberry cake mix	520	g
½ cup	vegetable oil	125	mL
4	eggs	4	

1. Generously grease a bundt pan or spray with a releasing agent.
2. Completely dissolve Jell-o in hot water in a large mixing bowl.
3. Add cake mix, oil and eggs and beat for 2 minutes at medium speed, until the batter is thick and creamy.
4. Pour the batter into the pan.
5. Microwave on MEDIUM, covered, for 12 minutes, in the bundt pan. If the cake is not done, repeat for 1 minute invervals until it is cooked. For an 8" (20 cm) cake pan, microwave each cake 4-5 minutes covered on MEDIUM.
6. Cool the cooked cake, invert onto plate and dust with sugar or glaze.

Glaze:

½ cup	icing sugar or powdered sugar	125	mL
1 tbsp.	milk or cream	15	mL
1 tsp.	lemon juice	5	mL

Blend until smooth and pour over the cake.
See photograph page 112.

Cherry Almond Cake

This is a pretty cake, suitable for Valentine's Day.

1	single-layer white cake mix, pouch size	250	g
¼ cup	amaretto	50	mL
	OR ½ tsp. almond flavoring	2	mL
1 cup	whipping cream	250	mL
2 tbsp.	sugar	30	mL
	red food coloring		
19 oz. can	cherry pie filling	540	mL
	slivered almonds		

1. Mix cake according to package directions.
2. Pour the batter, EXCEPT ½ cup (125 mL), into an 8" (20 cm) greased ring mold dish.*
3. To the reserved ½ cup (125 mL) of batter add a few drops of red food coloring.
4. Marble this through the batter in the cake pan.
5. Cover and microwave your cake on MEDIUM HIGH 4-6 minutes in a bundt pan or microwave ring mold.
6. Let stand until cool, then invert on to a pretty cake dish.
7. Fold the sugar into the whipped cream and add a few drops of red food coloring.
8. Ice the cake with the whipped cream and pile the cherry pie filling in the CENTRE of the cake.
9. Sprinkle the cake with almonds.

* If you do not have a ring mold, place a glass upright in the center of an 8" (20 cm) round cake pan and pour the batter around the glass.

Fresh Nectarine/Carrot Cake

¾ cup	brown sugar	175 mL
½ cup	oil	125 mL
2	eggs	2
1 tsp.	vanilla	5 mL
2 cups	flour	500 mL
2½ tsp.	baking powder	12 mL
1½ tsp.	cinnamon	7 mL
1½ cups	chopped nectarines	375 mL
1½ cups	finely grated carrot	375 mL
½ cup	chopped nuts	125 mL

1. Combine sugar, oil, eggs and vanilla. Beat until light and fluffy.
2. Sift dry ingredients together, add to wet ingredients and fold in nectarines, carrots and nuts.
3. Pour into 12-cup (3 L) bundt pan, cover with wax paper and microwave on HIGH 9-10 minutes. Frost with frosting below.

Tastes-Like-Cream-Cheese Frosting:

4 oz.	cream cheese or powdered sugar	125 g
3 tbsp.	butter	50 mL
½ cup	icing sugar	125 mL
1 tsp.	lemon juice	5 mL

1. Soften cream cheese and butter in microwave for 30-40 seconds, whip in icing sugar and lemon juice. Adjust consistancy by adding more or less icing sugar.

Fresh Fruit Coffee Cake

Batter:

1 cup	flour	250	mL
½ cup	sugar	125	mL
1 tbsp.	baking powder	15	mL
1 tsp.	salt	5	mL
2 tbsp.	butter or margarine	30	mL
1 cup	milk	250	mL
1	egg	1	

Streusel:

¼ cup	brown sugar	50	mL
¼ cup	oatmeal or granola	50	mL
¼ cup	flour	50	mL
1 tsp.	cinnamon	5	mL
½ cup	chopped nuts	125	mL
2 tbsp.	melted butter	10	mL
2 cups	fresh fruit, chopped	500	mL

1. To prepare batter, in a large mixing bowl combine flour, sugar, baking powder and salt.
2. Cut in butter until crumbly. Add milk and egg and mix well.
3. Combine all streusel ingredients, except the fruit.
4. Generously grease a bundt pan. Pour the batter into the bundt pan, layer the fruit over the batter and top with streusel mixture.
5. Cover and microwave on MEDIUM HIGH for 12 minutes. Let stand 10 minutes before turning out on to a plate. Cool.

Boston Cream Cake

A white cake with a creamy light filling topped with chocolate. A quick, easy cake for a special occasion.

9 oz.	single-layer white cake mix.	278 g

1. Prepare cake mix according to package directions. Place in a straight-sided micro-wave cake pan and microwave, covered, on MEDIUM HIGH 4-6 minutes.
2. Cool and slice horizontally through the middle.

Filling: Mock Cream

1½ tbsp.	cornstarch	22 mL
¾ cup	milk	175 mL
¼ cup	butter	50 mL
¼ cup	icing sugar or powdered sugar	50 mL
½ tsp.	vanilla	2 mL

3. Combine cornstarch and milk. Microwave on HIGH 2-3 minutes or until thickened.
4. Add remaining ingredients and beat or whisk until smooth. Cool and spread between the cake layers. Top with the following icing:

Icing:

¾ cup	chocolate chips	175 mL
2 tbsp.	butter	30 mL

5. Microwave on HIGH 1 to 1½ minutes, stirring after 1 minute. Pour over the top of the filled cake.

Microwave "6" Minute Frosting

Not nearly the hastle of 7-minute frosting and every bit as good!

1 cup	sugar	250 mL
⅓ cup	water	75 mL
⅛ tsp.	cream of tartar	1 mL
2	egg whites, stiffly beaten	2

1. Microwave the first 3 ingredients 4-4½ minutes on HIGH or until it reaches the softball stage. This is when the syrup slightly hardens into a soft ball when dropped into ice-cold water.
2. SLOWLY pour the hot syrup into the stiffly beaten egg whites, continue to beat until firm, about 2 minutes.

Variation: Use lime juice instead of water, and color with green food coloring. Spread on cooled cake and top with coconut for a tropical flavor.

Fudge Frosting

A thick creamy icing that tastes like good old-fashioned fudge. Excellent on brownies.

½ cup	butter or margarine	125 mL
½ cup	milk	125 mL
½ cup	sugar	125 mL
1 cup	semisweet chocolate chips	250 mL

1. Combine butter, milk and sugar in a medium-size bowl and microwave on HIGH for 5 minutes, stirring once after 2 minutes.
2. Add chocolate chips to sugar mixture, stir well and cool slightly.
3. Beat until thick and smooth. Icing will appear thin but will thicken when completely cool. Makes 2 cups (500 mL) of frosting for cakes or brownies.

Tastes-Like-Cream-Cheese-Frosting

A creamy frosting with the taste of cream cheese, not too sweet.

4 oz.	pkg. cream cheese	125 g
3 tbsp.	butter	50 mL
½ cup	icing sugar or powdered sugar	125 mL
1 tsp.	lemon juice	5 mL

1. Soften cream cheese and butter in microwave for 30-40 seconds, whip in icing sugar and lemon juice. Spread over cake. Adjust consistency with more or less icing sugar.

Creamy Caramel Frosting

2 tbsp.	butter*	30 mL
1 cup	icing sugar or powdered sugar	250 mL
¼ cup	evaporated milk	50 mL
1 tsp.	lemon juice	5 ml

1. Place butter in a 1-cup (250 mL) measure and microwave on HIGH 1-2 minutes or JUST until it starts to turn golden.
2. Add remaining ingredients, beat with a rotary beater or whisk until smooth and pour warm over cake.

*   Do not substitute butter with margarine.

Brown Sugar Frosting

This terrific icing will not harden.

1 cup	brown sugar	250 mL
5 tbsp.	butter	75 mL
¼ cup	milk	50 mL
1 tsp.	vanilla	5 mL
1 cup	icing sugar or powdered sugar	250 mL

1. Mix brown sugar, butter and milk in a medium-size bowl.
2. Microwave on HIGH for 5 minutes. Add vanilla.
3. Add icing sugar, beating until desired consistency is achieved.

Soft Cake Decorator's Frosting

This is similar to the frosting that most bakeries use on their cakes. It is not too sweet, yet full bodied.

1 cup	milk	250 mL
2 tbsp.	flour	30 mL
pinch	salt	pinch
½ cup	Crisco shortening	125 mL
½ cup	butter	125 mL
¾ cup	icing sugar or powdered sugar	175 mL

1. Whisk together the milk, flour and salt.
2. Place in a large bowl and microwave, uncovered, on HIGH 2-3 minutes or until thickened. Stir twice during cooking. Cool.
3. Beat in the remaining ingredients with a rotary beater until light and fluffy.

Light and Fruity Frosting

This is a delightfully light and fruity tasting frosting. Lovely served over angel food cake.

¾ cup	water	175 mL
3½ oz. pkg.	pineapple-flavored Jell-o*	100 g
1 envelope	whipped topping, whipped	1
	OR	
1 cup	whipping cream, stiffly beaten	250 mL

1. Place water in a 4-cup (1 L) measure and microwave, uncovered, on HIGH for 1½-2 minutes or until boiling.
2. Add Jell-o and stir until completely dissolved.
3. Place in the refrigerator JUST until the Jell-o is the consistency of egg whites.
4. Pour Jell-o into whipped cream and fold until well blended. Frost your cake immediately, otherwise the frosting will set.

* You may substitute with any other flavor Jell-o.

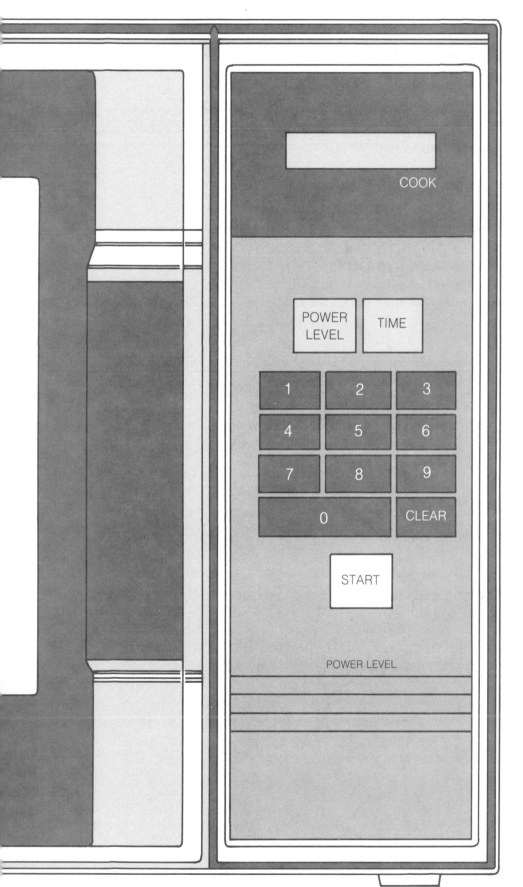

COOK

POWER LEVEL

TIME

1 2 3

4 5 6

7 8 9

0 CLEAR

START

POWER LEVEL

Good Old-Fashioned Apple Pie

Never-Fail Pastry:

Enough pastry for 5 single crusts. Can be frozen and is great to have on hand.

1 lb.	Crisco, chilled	500 mL
5 cups	flour	1.2 mL
1 tbsp.	sugar	15 mL
1 tsp.	baking powder	5 mL
2 tsp.	salt	10 mL
1	beaten egg	1
	cold tap water	
	juice of 1 lemon	

1. Cut shortening into flour and blend with pastry blender until mixture is crumbly, or place in food processor and process until the mixture is crumbly.
2. Add sugar, baking powder and salt. Toss lightly.
3. In 1-cup (250 mL) measure, beat egg and lemon juice. Add enough cold water to make exactly 1 cup (250 mL).
4. Add wet to dry ingredients, mix well. Form into 5 equal portions and wrap securely. FREEZE OVERNIGHT, or until needed.

Filling:

1 tbsp.	lemon juice	15 mL
6-8	tart cooking apples, cored and quartered	6-8
1 cup	sugar	250 mL
3 tbsp.	flour	45 mL
1 tbsp.	cinnamon	15 mL
¼ tsp.	nutmeg	1 mL
⅛ tsp.	salt	1 mL
2 tbsp.	butter	30 mL

1. Make a 9" (22 cm) pastry pie shell. Roll pastry between 2 sheets of floured wax paper for easy rolling.
2. Pour lemon juice over apples.
3. Toss apples lightly with the sugar, flour, cinnamon, nutmeg and salt mixture.
4. Place the apples in the UNBAKED BOTTOM SHELL. Dot with butter, and place crust over top. Slit top with sharp knife in several places. Brush with beaten egg white or melted butter.
5. Microwave on HIGH 15 minutes or until apples are tender.
6. PREHEAT CONVENTIONAL oven to 350°F (180°C) and bake pie for another 15 minutes until the top is golden in color.
   See photograph page 128.

Lemon Meringue Pie

Crust:

¼ cup	butter	50 mL
2 tbsp.	icing sugar or powdered sugar	30 mL
1¼ cups	fine graham cracker crumbs	300 mL
½ tsp.	cinnamon	2 mL
2 tbsp.	chopped pecans	30 mL

1. Microwave butter in 9" (22 cm) pie plate for 30 seconds.
2. Add remaining ingredients, and mix well.
3. Reserve ¼ cup (50 mL) for topping.
4. Gently press the remaining crumbs into the pie plate and microwave on MEDIUM HIGH for 1-1½ minutes.

Filling:

1	lemon pie filling mix OR lemon pie filling from scratch (see page 147 for lemon jelly).	1

1. Prepare the mix according to package directions except instead of cooking in a heavy saucepan, microwave, uncovered, on HIGH 5-6 minutes or until thickened. Stir occasionally.
2. Pour thickened filling into cooked crust. Cool.

Meringue:

3	egg whites	3
½ tsp.	cream of tartar	2 mL
½ cup	sugar	125 mL

1. Beat egg whites with cream of tartar until frothy.
2. Gradually add sugar and continue beating until the mixture is glossy and stiff peaks form. Do not overbeat.
3. Spread the meringue over the pie and microwave on MEDIUM for 2-3 minutes or until the meringue has set. Top with reserved crumbs.

* LEMON CHIFFON PIE: Fold the beaten egg whites directly into cooled lemon filling and refrigerate 1-2 hours before serving.

Mississippi Mud Pie

This is a real treat loaded with delicious calories. Start early in the day. Worth the effort!

¼ cup	melted butter	50 mL
⅓ cup	icing sugar or powdered sugar	75 mL
1½ cups	crushed chocolate wafers	375 mL

1. Combine crust ingredients and press GENTLY into a 9" (22 cm) pie plate. Microwave on MEDIUM HIGH 1½-2 minutes. Cool.

Filling:

3 cups	coffee ice cream	750 mL
10	caramel candies	10
1 tbsp.	milk	15 mL
¼ cup	butter or margarine	50 mL
¼ cup	milk	50 mL
½ cup	sugar	125 mL
¾ cup	chocolate chips	175 mL

2. Soften ice cream for 1 minute on LOW or until it can be easily spooned into crumb crust.
3. Freeze until ice cream is once again solid.
4. Place caramels and 1 tbsp. milk in a 1-cup (250 mL) measure. Microwave, uncovered, on HIGH for 30 seconds to 1 minute. Stir until smooth and completely melted. Cool slightly.
5. Pour over frozen ice cream and return to freezer.
6. Place butter, ¼ cup milk and sugar in bowl and microwave 1-2 minutes or until mixture comes to a full boil. Stir well.
7. Boil an additional 2½ minutes. Cool slightly.
8. Add chocolate chips and beat until mixture just starts to thicken. Pour over ice cream and return to freezer until ½ hour before serving.
9. ½ hour before serving, place the pie in the refrigerator to defrost slightly.

Grasshopper Pie

Chocolate Crumb Crust:

2 tbsp.	melted butter	30 mL
2 tbsp.	icing sugar or powdered sugar	30 mL
¾ cup	crushed chocolate wafers	175 mL
10-12	chocolate wafer halves	10-12

1. Combine butter, icing sugar and crumbs in a 9" (22 cm) plate. Press GENTLY on the bottom and up ¼" (½ cm) on the sides of the pie dish. Microwave, uncovered, on MEDIUM HIGH for 1½ minutes.
2. Carefully place the cookie halves around the inside of the pie dish with the rounded side up, creating a scalloped effect.

Filling:

½ cup	milk	125 mL
20	large marshmallows	20
1 cup	whipping cream	250 mL
1½ oz.	crème de menthe	45 mL
1½ oz.	crème de cacao	45 mL
	green food coloring, optional	

3. In large bowl melt milk and marshmallows on HIGH 2-3 minutes. Stir well and let mixture cool and thicken.
4. Whip cream until stiff peaks form and fold in liqueurs.
5. Carefully fold in the marshmallow mixture. Add a couple of drops of green food coloring if desired.
6. Place in crumb crust and chill for 2 hours. You may wish to garnish with some piped whipped cream and chocolate shavings.

Prize-Winning Raisin Cream Pie

1	precooked pie shell*	1	
1 cup	seedless raisins	250	mL
½ cup	water	125	mL
3 tbsp.	melted butter	45	mL
¾ cup	brown sugar	175	mL
2 cups	milk	500	mL
2 tbsp.	cornstarch	30	mL
⅛ tsp.	salt	1	mL
3	eggs, separated	3	
2 tsp.	vanilla	10	mL
6 tbsp.	sugar	90	mL
½ tsp.	cream of tartar	2	mL

1. Microwave raisins in water, on HIGH, for 2-3 minutes until they are plump. Drain and set aside.
2. Combine butter, brown sugar, milk, cornstarch and salt in a 4-cup (1 L) measure.
3. Microwave on HIGH 3-4 minutes, stirring frequently. Mixture will thicken.
4. Whisk egg yolks and add a small amount of hot liquid. Mix well and pour back into liquid.
5. Microwave on HIGH until mixture just returns to boil.
6. Fold in vanilla and DRAINED raisins. Pour into cooked pie shell.
7. Beat egg whites until frothy. Slowly add sugar and cream of tartar. Continue beating until stiff peaks form. Top pie with meringue.
8. Brown meringue in a preheated 450°F (230°C) oven for 5-7 minutes.

* See page 126 for pastry recipe. Microwave a single crust 4-6 minutes on MEDIUM HIGH. To keep shell from shrinking, flour generously the bottom and sides of a 9" (22 cm) pie plate and place on top of the uncooked shell which has been put into its pie plate for baking.

Southern Pecan Pie

1	prebaked pie shell*	1
¼ cup	melted butter	50 mL
1 cup	sugar	250 mL
¾ cup	light corn syrup	175 mL
3	eggs	3
1 tsp.	vanilla	5 mL
1¾ cups	pecans	425 mL

1. Combine butter, sugar and corn syrup in a large microwave bowl. Blend in eggs and vanilla and beat until light and fluffy.
2. Fold in pecans, pour into a baked pie shell and microwave, uncovered, on MEDIUM for 12-14 minutes or until center is set.
3. Cool completely before cutting.

* See page 126 for pastry recipe. Microwave a single crust 4-6 minutes on MEDIUM HIGH. To keep shell from shrinking, flour generously the bottom and sides of a 9" (22 cm) pie plate and place on top of the uncooked shell which has been put into its pie plate for baking.

Yogurt Lime Pie

Low in calories, high in nutritional value.

Crust:

1½ cups	finely crushed digestive biscuits or graham cracker crumbs (15)	375 mL
½ cup	melted butter	125 mL

Filling:

2 tbsp.	unflavored gelatin (2 envelopes)	2
½ cup	water	125 mL
¼ cup	sugar	50 mL
½ cup	lime juice	125 mL
¾ cup	water	175 mL
2 cups	plain yogurt	500 mL
2	egg whites, stiffly beaten	2

1. Combine crumbs with melted butter and press in a 9" (22 cm) pie plate. Set aside.
2. Combine gelatin, ½ cup (125 mL) water and sugar in a bowl and microwave on HIGH 25-35 seconds.
3. Stir in lime juice concentrate and ¾ cup (175 mL) water, whisk well and add yogurt. Whisk until completely blended.
4. Fold stiffly beaten egg whites into lime yogurt mixture and pour into crust. Refrigerate 2-3 hours or until set. Garnish with fresh lime slices if desired.

COOK

POWER LEVEL | TIME

1	2	3
4	5	6
7	8	9
0		CLEAR

START

POWER LEVEL

Lemon Cheesecake

Chocolate Crumb Crust:

¼ cup	melted butter	50 mL
⅓ cup	icing sugar or powdered sugar	75 mL
1½ cups	graham wafer crumbs	375 mL
2 tbsp.	cocoa	30 mL

1. Combine the crust ingredients and press GENTLY into the bottom ONLY of a 10" (25 cm) Pyrex pie plate.*
2. Microwave on MEDIUM HIGH for 1½-2 minutes.

Filling:

14 oz.	cream cheese	400 g
¼ cup	sugar	50 mL
2	eggs	2
1 tsp.	vanilla	5 mL
	juice of 1 lemon	1
1 tbsp.	grated lemon peel	15 mL
1 cup	sour cream	250 mL

3. Soften cream cheese in bowl on MEDIUM for 1 minute or more if necessary.
4. Beat in sugar, blend in eggs, vanilla, lemon juice, peel and sour cream.
5. Pour into prepared crust.
6. Microwave on MEDIUM HIGH for 15 minutes or until the center is almost firm.**

* Mini Cheesecakes: Eliminate crust and place a chocolate cookie in a paper muffin liner, placed in a microwave muffin pan. Fill half full with filling, microwave on MEDIUM 5 minutes per 6 cupcakes.

** If you have difficulty with centers undercooking, elevate on a rack or put a soup bowl or small casserole UPRIGHT under the middle of the pie plate. You could also cover the cheese cake with a lid or inverted pie plate until the last minute of cooking.

Lightweight Cheesecake

Graham Wafer Crust:

1½ cups	crushed graham wafers or crumbs	375 mL
⅓ cup	icing sugar or powdered sugar	75 mL
½ cup	butter or margarine, melted	125 mL

1. Combine graham crumbs and icing sugar. Mix well.
2. Add melted butter and press into a 9" (22 cm) Pyrex pie plate, or 8" x 8" (20 x 20 cm) square glass cake pan.
3. Microwave on MEDIUM HIGH 1½ minutes. Set aside to cool.

Filling:

1	envelope plain gelatin	1
½ cup	water	125 mL
¼ cup	lemon juice	50 mL
14 oz. can	crushed pineapple	398 mL
2 tbsp.	sugar	30 mL
2 cups	2% creamed cottage cheese	500 mL
2	eggs, separated, whites stiffly-beaten	2

4. Combine gelatin, water and lemon juice in 1 cup (250 mL) measure and microwave on HIGH for 20-30 seconds.
5. Place in freezer for 10 minutes to cool quickly. Do not set.
6. Combine crushed pineapple, sugar, cottage cheese and egg yolks. Mix in blender until smooth.
7. Fold in stiffly-beaten egg whites, add to gelatin mixture and pour into cooked crust. Refrigerate for 1-2 hours, or until set.

Party Dessert

The simple things in life are often the best!

Crust:

17	chocolate-coated graham crackers*	17

1. Crush the crackers and press ALL but ½ cup of them into a 9" (22 cm) square pan.

Filling:

6 oz. pkg.	lemon Jell-o powder, or any flavor you wish	170 g
1 tbsp.	gelatin	15 mL
1 cup	boiling water	250 mL
1 tbsp.	lemon juice	15 mL
1 quart	vanilla ice cream	1 L

2. Dissolve Jell-o and gelatin in boiling water.
3. Mix in lemon juice.
4. Soften ice cream by microwaving it on MEDIUM HIGH for 1 to 1½ minutes, or until soft enough to stir into the Jell-o.
5. Blend ice cream and Jell-o until smooth.
6. Pour carefully over crust and top with the ½ cup of reserved graham crumbs.
7. REFRIGERATE at least 6 hours. (24 hours is better)

* If you do not have chocolate-coated graham wafers line the pan with plain graham crackers. Microwave 1 cup (250 mL) semi-sweet chocolate chips with 2 tbsp. (30 mL) butter and 1 tbsp. (15 mL) milk on HIGH for 1-1½ minutes. Stir well and pour over graham crackers. Let cool and set in the refrigerator. Use this as your crust. Top the dessert with plain graham cracker crumbs.

Ann's Blender Mousse

Simple. Elegant. Always a hit!

1 cup	water	250 mL
1 cup	chocolate chips	250 mL
4	eggs	4
2 tbsp.	icing sugar or powdered sugar	30 mL
⅓ cup	Kahlúa liqueur* See page 14 for recipe.	75 mL
1 tbsp.	unflavored gelatin (1 envelope)	15 mL
½ cup	whipped cream	125 mL

Ann's Blender Mousse (cont'd)

1. Place the water in 2-cup (500 mL) measure and microwave, uncovered, on HIGH 1-2 minutes or just until boiling.
2. Place chocolate chips in blender, add boiling water, gelatin, eggs (1 at a time), and sugar blending continuously.
3. Add liqueur, blend well and pour into serving glasses. Cool and garnish with whipped cream, or cool and fold in ½ cup whipped cream.

* Other liqueurs that we recommend are: Grand Marnier, crème de menthe or amaretto.

White Chocolate Mousse with Raspberry Champagne Sauce

6 oz.	white chocolate, cut into small chunks	170 g
2 cups	whipping cream	500 mL
2 tsp.	lemon peel	10 mL
	fresh mint for garnish	

1. In small bowl combine white chocolate and ¼ cup (50 mL) whipping cream. Microwave on MEDIUM for 2-3 minutes or until mixture is creamy and smooth.
2. Cool and stir in lemon peel.
3. In large bowl beat remainder of whipping cream until stiff.
4. Carefully fold remaining whipped cream into cooled chocolate mixture.
5. Into serving bowls or goblets, ladle ⅓ cup (75 mL) Raspberry Champagne Sauce, below. Top with a generous serving of mousse.

Raspberry Champagne Sauce:*

1½ cups	raspberry juice concentrate	375 mL
2 cups	champagne, pink or white	500 mL
4 tbsp.	raspberry flavored liqueur or syrup	50 mL
2 tbsp.	sugar	30 mL

1. Combine all ingredients in an 8-cup (2 L) bowl.
2. Microwave, uncovered, on HIGH for 20 to 25 minutes, or until thickened slightly.
3. Store in a glass container.

* Sauce can be served with the mousse either at room temperature or warmed slightly. It is also excellent drizzled over vanilla ice cream.
For a quick and easy dessert, slice pound cake, top with vanilla ice cream and drizzle with sauce.
See photograph page 112.

Caramel Mocha Delight

An easy, delicious dessert that is sure to be "cleaned up".

6 oz. pkg.	butterscotch pudding mix (DO NOT USE INSTANT)	170	g
1½ cups	water	375	ml
½ tsp.	instant coffee granules	2	mL
½ tsp.	maple flavoring	2	mL
1	large angel food cake*	1	
4	Coffee Crisp chocolate bars	4-47	g
2 cups	whipping cream, whipped	500	mL
½ cup	coffee liqueur	125	mL

1. Combine pudding mix and water. Microwave, uncovered, on HIGH 4-5 minutes, stirring twice. Mixture will be thick and clear. Stir in instant coffee and maple flavoring. Set aside to cool.
2. Tear the cake into bite-size pieces. Crush the Coffee Crisp chocolate bars.
3. Fold HALF of the whipped cream into the cooled pudding. Stir in the liqueur and fold in the cake pieces.
4. Spoon half of the cake mixture into a large glass bowl. Sprinkle with half of the crushed chocolate bar.
5. Repeat with the other half of the cake mixture and the other half of the chocolate bar.
6. Top with remaining whipped cream.
7. Refrigerate 2-3 hours before serving.

* An angel food cake can be prepared very quickly in the microwave. However, it is more moist than a conventionally cooked angel food cake. The microwave method is superb for desserts such as this, because of the speed of cooking. See page 116 for directions for microwaving an Angel Food Cake.

Crunchy Fruit Crisp

5	apples, peeled and chopped	5	
¼ cup	crushed graham crackers	50	mL
2 tbsp.	flour	30	mL
¼ cup	brown sugar, packed	50	mL
¼ tsp.	cinnamon	1	mL
¼ cup	granola	50	mL
¼ cup	melted butter or margarine	50	mL

Crunchy Fruit Crisp (cont'd)

1. Place apples in a 4-cup (1 L) casserole.
2. Combine remaining ingredients EXCEPT the butter.
3. Add butter to dry ingredients and mix until crumbly.
4. Spread over apples and pat gently.
5. Microwave on HIGH for 6 to 8 minutes, or until apples are tender.

* For a cheesy apple flavor, combine ¼ cup (50 mL) shredded Cheddar to crumbly mixture.

Light and Fluffy Tapioca Cream

1	egg, separated	1
2 tbsp.	sugar	30 mL
3 tbsp.	tapioca	45 mL
2 cups	milk	500 mL
2 tbsp.	sugar (second amount)	30 mL
1 tsp.	vanilla	5 mL

1. Beat egg white until foamy, add sugar and continue beating until stiff peaks form. Set aside.
2. Combine remaining ingredients except vanilla in a 1-quart (1 L) casserole.
3. Microwave on HIGH 4-6 minutes until mixture comes to a full boil. Boil an additional 2 minutes. Stir at least twice.
4. Fold in beaten egg white and vanilla and pour into serving dishes. Garnish with fresh fruit if desired.

Crunchy Ras'n Rhuberry Slice

Serve warm with ice cream.

Batter:

1 cup	flour	250	mL
½ cup	sugar	125	mL
1 tbsp.	baking powder	15	mL
1 tsp.	salt	5	mL
2 tbsp.	butter or margarine	30	mL
1 cup	milk	250	mL
1	egg	1	

Topping:

1 cup	sugar	250	mL
⅓ cup	flour	75	mL
1 cup	chopped pecans	250	mL
½ tsp.	cinnamon	2	mL
½ cup	butter or margarine	125	mL
½ tsp.	nutmeg	2	mL
4 cups	fresh rhubarb, chopped	1	L
	OR		
2 cups	frozen, thawed and drained rhubarb	500	mL
3 oz. pkg.	raspberry or strawberry Jell-o	85	g

1. To prepare batter, in a large mixing bowl combine flour, sugar, baking powder and salt.
2. Cut in butter until crumbly. Add milk and egg and mix well.
3. Pour equal proportions of batter into 2 greased 8" (20 cm) round microwave cake pans.
4. Prepare topping by mixing the 6 topping ingredients well with a fork. Set aside.
5. Spoon rhubarb over top of batter and sprinkle with dry Jell-o, then sprinkle with the topping.
6. Microwave each dish separately on MEDIUM for 4 to 5 minutes, uncovered.

Dessert Crêpes

For dessert crêpes add ¼ cup (50 mL) icing sugar to basic crêpe recipe on page 32. Cook as directed.

Crêpe Suzettes:

The fame and popularity of this elegant dessert makes the word Suzette synonymous with crêpe.

12	dessert crêpes	12	
6	sugar cubes	6	
1	orange	1	
¼ cup	butter	50	mL
½ cup	sifted icing sugar or powdered sugar	125	mL
1 tsp.	grated orange rind	5	mL
½ cup	orange juice	125	mL
1 tsp.	lemon juice	5	mL
⅓ cup	Grand Marnier, or any orange liqueur	75	mL
1	thinly-sliced orange, for garnish	1	
¼ cup	brandy	50	mL

1. Rub sugar cubes into the skin of the orange until the cubes are yellow. Set aside.
2. Melt butter in 1-quart (1 L) casserole, blend in icing sugar. Stir in rind, orange juice, lemon juice and sugar cubes.
3. Microwave, uncovered, on HIGH 2-3 minutes. Stir frequently to dissolve sugar cubes completely. Cool slightly.
4. Add liqueur, stir until blended.
5. Fold crêpes into quarters. Place in chafing dish or colorful serving platter. Pour sauce over all. Garnish with orange slices.
6. Pour brandy into a 1-cup (250 mL) measure, microwave, uncovered, on HIGH 30 seconds. Immediately pour heated brandy over crêpes. Set alight and serve after flames subside.

English Trifle

Well worth the effort!

1	sponge or pound cake	1	
4	eggs, separated	4	
1½ cups	light cream	375	mL
½ cup	sherry, rum or brandy	125	mL
¼ cup	white sugar	50	mL
20 oz. pkg.	frozen raspberries	500	g
¼ cup	sherry	50	mL
1 cup	whipping cream	250	mL
¼ cup	icing sugar or powdered sugar	50	mL
¼ cup	toasted almonds	50	mL
5	maraschino cherries	5	

1. Break cake into bite-size pieces and arrange HALF in the bottom of a deep glass bowl.
2. Beat egg yolks until light and pale in color. Set aside.
3. Place light cream in bowl and microwave, uncovered, on HIGH 1½-2 minutes to scald.
4. Add liquor and white sugar and mix well.
5. Microwave on MEDIUM for 2-3 minutes, stirring frequently.
6. Add some of the hot mixture to the egg yolks, and return this to the hot liquid. Microwave on MEDIUM HIGH 1-2 minutes or until mixture just begins to boil. Stir frequently. DO NOT BOIL this mixture or the yolks will cook separately and curdle.
7. Beat egg whites until stiff peaks form and fold into thickened, cooled milk mixture.
8. Spread ½ of fruit on the cake, then top with ½ the custard mixture.
9. Repeat the layers.
10. Pour second amount of liquor over all.
11. Whip cream with icing sugar until stiff. Spread over top. Decorate with toasted almonds and cherries.
12. Refrigerate 12 hours so flavors have a chance to blend, and you have a chance to rest!!

Bread Pudding with Whiskey Sauce

¼ cup	butter	50 mL
⅓ cup	white sugar	75 mL
	juice and rind of half a lemon	
5-6 slices	bread, cubed	5-6
1 cup	raisins, rinsed in hot water	250 mL
1 cup	milk	250 mL
3	eggs, well beaten	3
½ tsp.	cinnamon	2 mL

1. Combine butter, sugar, lemon juice and rind in 4-cup (1 L) casserole.
2. Microwave on HIGH 1-2 minutes, stir.
3. Place cubed bread and raisins in butter sauce and coat evenly.
4. Whisk milk and eggs and pour milk mixture over the bread. DO NOT STIR. Sprinkle with cinnamon.
5. Microwave, uncovered, 7 to 8 minutes on HIGH, or until completely set.
6. Serve warm with New Orleans Whiskey Sauce, below.

New Orleans Whiskey Sauce:

This was definitely worth the trip to New Orleans!

¼ cup	butter	50 mL
½ cup	sugar	125 mL
1	egg	1
1 tbsp.	whiskey (Canadian or Bourbon)	30 mL

1. Combine butter and sugar and microwave, uncovered on HIGH for 1 to 1½ minutes to completely melt butter and sugar. Beat well. Cool slightly.
2. Whisk in egg and whiskey.
3. Microwave on MEDIUM to MEDIUM HIGH 1 minute stirring every 20-30 seconds or until sauce thickens. DO NOT overcook as sauce will easily curdle. Use a lower power level if necessary.

Apple Pudding

3 cups	thinly sliced apples	750	mL
½ cup	white sugar	125	mL
1 tsp.	cinnamon	5	mL
1 cup	white flour	250	mL
2 tsp.	baking powder	10	mL
	pinch salt	1	mL
⅓ cup	white sugar (second amount)	75	mL
1	egg	1	
½ cup	milk	125	mL
3 tbsp.	butter	50	mL
½ cup	brown sugar	125	mL
1 tsp.	cinnamon	5	mL
1 tbsp.	hot water	15	mL

1. Place apples in an 8-cup (2 L) casserole, sprinkle with ½ cup (125 mL) sugar and the cinnamon.
2. Combine flour, baking powder, salt, ⅓ cup (75 mL) sugar, egg and milk. Beat for 2 minutes.
3. Pour this mixture OVER the apples.
4. Combine butter, brown sugar, cinnamon, and water. Sprinkle over the doughy mixture.
5. Microwave on HIGH, uncovered, for 5-8 minutes or until the apples are fork tender. Serve with ice cream or Apple Cream, below.

Apple Cream:

3 tbsp.	cornstarch	45	mL
1½ cups	apple juice	375	mL
½ cup	butter	125	mL
½ cup	icing sugar or powdered sugar	125	mL
1 tsp.	rum extract	5	mL
	OR		
1 tbsp.	amber rum (optional)	15	mL

1. Combine cornstarch and apple juice in a 4-cup (1 L) measure or bowl and microwave on HIGH 3-4 minutes or until slightly thickened.
2. Add butter, icing sugar and rum extract. Whisk to blend well.
3. Pour the warm sauce over the apple pudding.

Creamy Rice Pudding

1 cup	rice	250 mL
2 cups	water	500 mL
½ cup	raisins	125 mL
1 tsp.	cinnamon	5 mL
½ tsp.	ground nutmeg	2 mL

1. Place rice and water in 12-cup (3 L) casserole, cover with boiling water and microwave on MEDIUM for 15-18 minutes. Keep covered and let stand 5 minutes.
2. Add raisins, cinnamon and nutmeg. Fold Mock Cream, below, into rice.

Mock Cream:

3 tbsp.	cornstarch	45 mL
1½ cups	milk	375 mL
½ cup	butter	125 mL
½ cup	icing sugar or powdered sugar	125 mL
½ tsp.	vanilla	2 mL

3. Combine cornstarch and milk in 8-cup (2 L) casserole and microwave on HIGH 2-3 minutes or until thickened.
4. Add butter, icing sugar and vanilla. Beat until creamy.
5. Combine with rice, reheat 2-3 minutes on HIGH, serve warm.

Creamy Chocolate Pudding

No preservatives, quick and more economical than canned puddings. The icing sugar gives a real velvety texture to this pudding and its variation, which is just one of many you can adapt to this recipe. Kids love it!

3 tbsp.	cornstarch	50 mL
1½ cups	milk	375 mL
2 tbsp.	cocoa	30 mL
½ cup	icing sugar or powdered sugar	125 mL
½ cup	margarine or butter	125 mL

1. Combine the first 4 ingredients, whisk and microwave, uncovered, on HIGH for 3-4 minutes or until thickened.
2. Add butter and stir until melted. Pour into serving bowls. Refrigerate until set.

   Chocolate Banana Pudding: Slice 2-3 ripe bananas into cooked pudding, top with a maraschino cherry or a dollop of whipped cream.

Cherry or Blueberry Delight Dessert

Crust:

1¼ cups	fine graham cracker crumbs	300	mL
⅓ cup	melted butter	75	mL
2 tbsp.	brown sugar	30	mL
1 tsp.	cinnamon	5	mL

1. Mix the above ingredients. Reserve ⅓ cup (75 mL) for topping. Spread the remaining crumbs in the bottom of a large square dish. Microwave on HIGH for 2½ to 3 minutes.

Filling:

½ cup	milk	125	mL
32	large marshmallows	32	
1 cup	whipping cream, whipped	250	mL
1½ cups	cherry or blueberry pie filling, OR homemade filling*	375	mL

1. Combine milk and marshmallows in large bowl and microwave on HIGH for 2½-3 minutes or until the marshmallows are melted. Stir until smooth and cool.
2. Fold in whipped cream.
3. Pour half of this mixture over the crust. Carefully spread the pie filling OVER the top of the whipped cream mixture.
4. Spread the remaining half of the whipped cream over the pie filling.
5. Sprinkle with the remaining crumb mixture. Chill for at least 1 hour.

*Homemade Fruit Pie Filling

19 oz. can	sweetened fruit	540	mL
2 tbsp.	cornstarch	30	mL
1 tsp.	lemon juice	5	mL

1. Drain fruit, chop finely, and set aside. Combine cornstarch and lemon juice with the liquid. Microwave on HIGH 2-3 minutes or until thickened, stirring twice. Fold in fruit and use in place of canned filling.
2. Cool completely before using.

Lemon Jelly

A family favorite for generations. No need for a double boiler. Super for a tart or pie filling.

3	eggs, well beaten	3
1 cup	sugar	250 mL
dash	salt	1 mL
¼ cup	melted butter	50 mL
	juice of 3 lemons	3
	OR ¼ cup bottled lemon juice	50 mL
1 tsp.	lemon rind (optional)	5 mL

1. Combine all ingredients in 4-cup (1 L) measure.
2. Microwave on HIGH 2 minutes, stirring once, or until mixture is thick and clear.
3. Cool and refrigerate until ready to use.

   This jelly can be used as a filling for cupcakes. Make regular white cupcakes and slice off the top. Make a well in the cupcake and fill with 1 tbsp. (15 mL) of jelly. Place the top back on and sprinkle with icing sugar.

Hawaiian Coconut Pudding

1½ cups	flaked sweetened coconut	375 mL
4 cups	milk	1 L
½ cup	cornstarch	125 mL
4 tbsp.	sugar	60 mL
14 oz. can	crushed pineapple, drained	398 mL

1. Combine coconut and milk in electric blender and blend for 5 minutes. Strain out coconut pieces through a double thickness of cheesecloth or a nylon (preferably clean!). Reserve coconut.
2. Combine cornstarch, and sugar and gradually add the coconut milk, stirring to blend.
3. Microwave 3-4½ minutes stirring occasionally until mixture is thickened.
4. Fold in pineapple and pour into individual serving dishes and top with toasted coconut.

Orange Julep Chiffon

This dessert requires a 9" (22 cm) springform pan.

1¼ cups	digestive cookie or graham cracker crumbs (12 crackers)	300	mL
⅓ cup	melted butter	75	mL
2	small pkgs. Orange Julep Jell-o powder	2-85	g
¼ cup	granulated sugar	50	mL
2	large eggs, separated, whites stiffly beaten	2	
1 cup	orange juice	250	mL
1 cup	whipping cream	250	mL
2 tbsp.	icing sugar or powdered sugar	25	mL
2 cups	Philadelphia cream cheese, softened	500	mL

1. Combine cookie crumbs and melted butter and press into the bottom of a 9" (22 cm) springform pan.
2. Combine Jell-o powder, granulated sugar, egg yolks and orange juice in a 4-cup measure, whisk until blended.
3. Microwave on MEDIUM HIGH 2½-3 minutes. Whisk after each minute, until slightly thickened.
4. Cool in the refrigerator for 10 minutes. Beat in cream cheese.
5. Beat whipping cream until stiff, add icing sugar.
6. Fold egg whites into whipped cream.
7. Fold whipped cream mixture into Jell-o mixture. Spoon onto crust, and chill 1-2 hours. Garnish with orange slices. Serves 12.
   See photograph page 160.

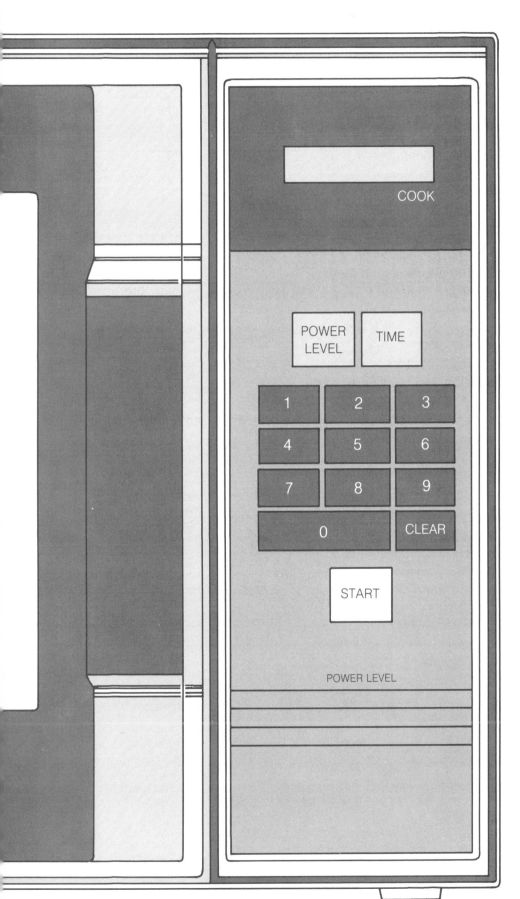

Squares and Candy

Krispy Krunch Bars

One of Grandma's torn and tattered recipes!

¾ cup	corn syrup	175	mL
¾ cup	brown sugar	175	mL
¾ cup	peanuts	175	mL
½ tsp.	vanilla	2	mL
pinch	salt	1	mL
1 tbsp.	butter	15	mL
2 cups	cornflakes	500	mL
2 cups	rice krispies	500	mL

1. Microwave syrup and brown sugar for 5 minutes on HIGH or until mixture is bubbling and sugar is completely dissolved.
2. Mix in peanuts, vanilla, salt and butter.
3. Combine the cornflakes and rice krispies and pour over the peanut mixture. Mix until evenly coated.
4. Pour into a greased 9" x 13" (22 x 33 cm) pan. Cut into squares. Store in airtight container. Serve at room temperature.

Hershey's Brownies

The best brownies around! Deliciously rich and moist.

½ cup	soft butter or margarine	125	mL
1 cup	sugar	250	mL
4	eggs	4	
10 oz. can	Hershey's chocolate ice cream syrup*	284	mL
1 cup	flour	250	mL
½ tsp.	baking powder	2	mL
½ tsp.	vanilla	2	mL
½ cup	chopped walnuts, optional	125	mL

1. Beat margarine, sugar and eggs until light and fluffy.
2. Add remaining ingredients EXCEPT walnuts. Beat until smooth.
3. Add walnuts and pour into two 9" (22 cm) pie plates or one large circular microwave dish approximately 10" (30 cm) in diameter.
4. Cover with a plate and microwave on HIGH 5-6 minutes for each 9" (22 cm) pie plate or 8-10 minutes for a larger dish. Ice with Fudge Frosting, see page 122.

* If you don't have Hershey Chocolate Syrup, you can substitute with 1¼ cups of Fancy Fudge Sauce, page 107.
See photograph page 160.

150

Chewy Almond Bars

1½ cups	graham cracker crumbs	375 mL
¾ cups	finely chopped almonds	175 mL
10 oz. can	sweetened condensed milk*	300 mL
¼ cup	melted butter	50 mL
½ cup	semisweet chocolate chips	125 mL
¼ tsp.	salt	5 mL

1. In an 8-cup (2 L) bowl combine all ingredients.
2. Pour into a well greased round pie plate.
3. Microwave covered on HIGH 5-7 minutes until bars are no longer moist. UNCOVER IMMEDIATELY. Let stand 10 minutes.

*

Peanut Butter/Chocolate Chip/ Marshmallow Bars

After you get past the name, the rest is easy.

6 oz. pkg.	chocolate chips	175 g
6 oz. pkg.	butterscotch chips	175 g
½ cup	butter or margarine	125 mL
1 tsp.	vanilla	5 mL
1 cup	peanut butter	250 mL
½ cup	coconut	125 mL
¾ cup	walnuts	175 mL
6 oz. pkg.	colored marshmallows	175 g

1. Mix chocolate chips, butterscotch chips and butter in a large mixing bowl.
2. Microwave on MEDIUM for 2½ to 3 minutes, stirring well after 1 minute.
3. When chips have melted, stir in remaining ingredients.
4. Pour into a greased 9 x 13" (22 x 33 cm) pan and cool.
5. When completely cooled, cut into squares. Freezes well.
   See photograph page 160.

Pineapple Squares

Crust:

½ cup	butter	125	mL
¼ cup	sugar	50	mL
1¼ cups	all-purpose flour	300	mL

Filling:

1 cup	brown sugar	250	mL
1 cup	drained crushed pineapple (reserve juice)	250	mL
½ tsp.	almond flavoring	2	mL
¼ tsp.	salt	1	mL
½ tsp.	baking powder	2	mL
2 tbsp.	flour	25	mL
½ cup	walnuts	125	mL

Icing:

2 cups	icing sugar or powdered sugar	500	mL
3 tbsp.	butter	45	mL
1 tbsp.	milk	15	mL
1½ tsp.	reserved pineapple juice	7	mL

1. Combine crust ingredients until crumbly and GENTLY press into the bottom of a greased 9 x 9" (23 x 23 cm) glass dish.
2. Beat all filling ingredients together and spread over the crust.
3. Microwave, uncovered, on MEDIUM HIGH 6-7 minutes or until completely set. Cool.
4. Combine icing ingredients and beat until smooth and well blended. Ice when squares are completely cool. This also may be topped with ½ cup (125 mL) toasted coconut. See photograph page 160.

Sweet Ruth Squares

Similar to Nanaimo Bars.

30	graham wafers	30
½ cup	margarine	125 mL
½ cup	milk	125 mL
1 cup	brown sugar	250 mL
1 cup	chopped nuts	250 mL
1 cup	fine coconut	250 mL
½ cup	chocolate chips	125 mL
1 cup	graham wafer crumbs	250 mL

1. Line graham wafers in bottom of 12 x 9" (30 x 22 cm) casserole. You may need to do some cutting to make them fit.
2. Combine the next 3 ingredients in a 4-cup (1 L) measure and microwave on HIGH 2-3 minutes or just until boiling.
3. Combine the next 4 ingredients and add them to the boiling mixture.
4. Pour over top of the graham wafers.
5. Frost with frosting below.

Frosting:

2 tbsp.	soft margarine	30 mL
1 cup	icing sugar or powdered sugar	250 mL
1 tbsp.	Bird's Custard Powder or Vanilla Pudding Mix	15 mL
2 tbsp.	milk or cream	30 mL
1 tsp.	vanilla	5 mL

1. Combine the above and beat with rotary beater until smooth and slightly runny. You may need to add more milk.
2. Pour over the squares and refrigerate until set.

Rice Krispie Squares

A great recipe for kids to prepare and easy clean up for mom or dad.

¼ cup	butter or margarine	50 mL
4 cups	miniature marshmallows	1 L
6 cups	rice krispies or Fruit Loops	1.5 L

1. Place marshmallows and butter in your LARGEST microwave safe bowl. Microwave on HIGH for 2 minutes, stirring twice.
2. Add rice krispies or Fruit Loops and stir well. Pour into a greased 12" x 9" (30 x 22 cm) dish. Cool and cut into squares.

* For a variation, melt ½ cup (125 mL) chocolate chips with 2 tbsp. (30 mL) butter and pour over the squares after step 2 above.

Peanut Butter Rice Krispie Squares

⅔ cup	sweetened condensed milk*	150 mL
¼ cup	peanut butter	50 mL
¼ cup	corn syrup	50 mL
½ cup	brown sugar	125 mL
4 cups	rice krispies	1 L

1. Mix all ingredients EXCEPT rice krispies in a large bowl.
2. Microwave, uncovered, on MEDIUM HIGH for 3-6 minutes, stirring occasionally until the mixture is the consistency of pudding.
3. Add rice krispies and stir until well coated. Pour into a greased 9" x 9" (22 cm) pan and chill until set. Cut into squares.

*

Chocolate Chip Granola Bars

This easy recipe can be changed to whatever suits your taste. By omitting the 1 cup (250 mL) of chocolate chips you can add 1 cup (250 mL) of your favorite dried fruit or nuts to make the granola bars of your choice.

½ cup	honey or corn syrup	125 mL
½ cup	packed brown sugar	125 mL
1 cup	chocolate chips	250 mL
2 tsp.	vanilla	10 mL
2 cups	granola cereal (See page 31 for Homemade Granola)	500 mL
1 cup	Kellogg's Raisin Crisp or Bran Flakes	250 mL

1. Combine honey and brown sugar in a 4-cup (1 L) measure and microwave on HIGH 1-2 minutes until mixture begins to boil. Boiling for longer period of time (i.e. 30 sec. to 1 minute) will make the bars more crisp.

2. Combine with remaining ingredients and press into an 8 x 8" (22 cm) square pan. Cut into bars and refrigerate until set.

If you should choose to double the recipe, microwave the honey/brown sugar mixture for 2-3 minutes, or until it just comes to a boil.

APRICOT & ALMOND GRANOLA BARS

Follow directions given above omitting the chocolate chips. Add ½ cup (125 mL) slivered or flaked almonds and ½ cup (125 mL) finely chopped dried apricots.

APPLE CINNAMON GRANOLA BARS

Follow directions given above omitting the chocolate chips. Add 1 cup (250 mL) chopped dried apple and 1 tsp. (5 mL) cinammon.

CRUNCHY PEANUT BUTTER GRANOLA BARS

Follow directions given above, omitting the chocolate chips. Add 1 cup (250 mL) crunchy peanut butter or 1 cup (250 mL) plain peanut butter and ¼ cup (50 mL) crushed peanuts.

See photograph page 160.

155

Fantastic Fudge

"Ye Ole Microwave does a great job on this one."

2 cups	sugar	500 mL
¾ cup	butter	175 mL
⅔ cup	evaporated milk	150 mL
8 oz. pkg.	semisweet chocolate chips*	250 g
1	jar of marshmallow cream	200 g
	OR	
	15 large marshmallows	15
1 tsp.	vanilla	5 mL
1 cup	chopped nuts	250 mL

1. Combine sugar, butter and milk in 8-cup (2 L) casserole.
2. Microwave on HIGH, UNCOVERED, 4½ to 5 minutes or until the mixture just begins to boil. Stir well.
3. Microwave on HIGH another 5½ minutes.
4. Stir in chocolate chips, marshmallow cream, vanilla and nuts. Stir well.
5. Pour into greased 12 x 8" (30 x 20 cm) baking dish and cool until set.

   Makes 3½ lbs. (1.75 kg) of calorie-loaded delicious fudge.

* Instead of chocolate chips you could use butterscotch chips, chocolate mint chips, peanut butter chips, or orange chocolate chips.

Chocolate Mint Fudge

2 cups	sugar	500 mL
3 tbsp.	butter	45 mL
1 cup	evaporated milk	250 mL
1 cup	mini marshmallows	250 mL
1½ cups	semisweet chocolate chips	375 mL
⅔ cup	chopped pecans or walnuts	150 mL
1 tsp.	peppermint extract	5 mL

1. Combine first 4 ingredients and microwave on HIGH for 5 minutes, stirring only once.
2. Add remaining ingredients and microwave on MEDIUM HIGH power for another 5 minutes.
3. Remove from microwave and beat with wooden spoon for 3-5 minutes until fudge looks glossy. Pour into an 8" (20 cm) square pan and refrigerate until set.

Deep Chocolate Pecan Fudge

4 cups	icing sugar or powdered sugar	1	L
1½ cups	cocoa, unsweetened	375	mL
1 cup	butter	250	mL
⅔ cup	milk	175	mL
1 cup	pecans or walnuts	250	mL
2 tbsp.	vanilla	30	mL

1. Sift icing sugar and cocoa together in a large bowl. Set aside.
2. In a separate glass bowl combine butter and milk. Microwave uncovered on HIGH 2-3 minutes or until the butter has completely melted. Stir.
3. Pour melted butter and milk evenly over cocoa/icing sugar mixture. DO NOT STIR.
4. Microwave, uncovered, 4-6 minutes or until bubbling.
5. Stir in pecans and vanilla. Beat until smooth and pour into a greased 8" (20 cm) square baking pan. Refrigerate until set.
   See photograph page 160.

Notes:

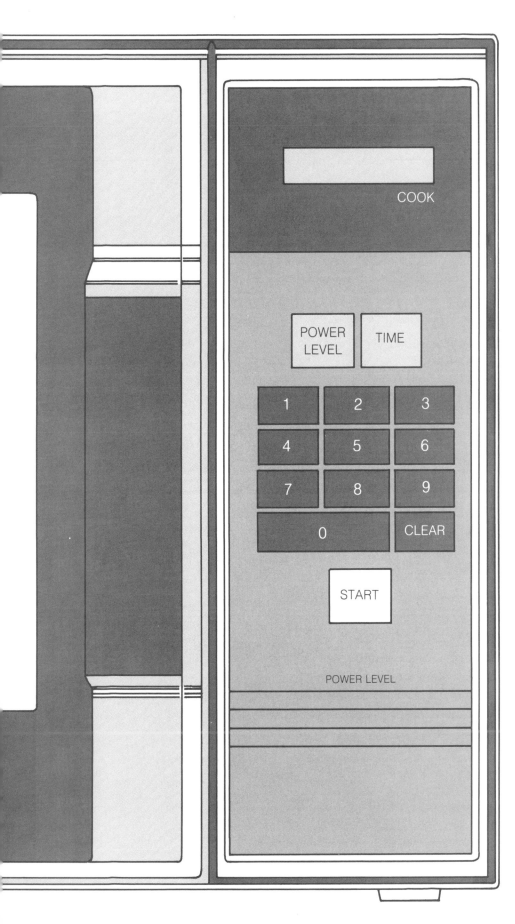

COOK

POWER LEVEL

TIME

1	2	3
4	5	6
7	8	9
0		CLEAR

START

POWER LEVEL

Kiwi Freezer Jam

6	medium-size kiwi fruits	6
½ cup	sugar	125 mL
1 tbsp.	lemon juice	15 mL
2 tbsp.	Slim Set	30 mL
¾ cup	water	175 mL

1. Crush kiwi fruit and add sugar. Microwave on HIGH 2-3 minutes or until boiling.
2. Add lemon juice, Slim Set and water. Microwave 3-4 minutes or until mixture returns to a boil.
3. Pour into a clean glass jar and store in the refrigerator. Yields about 2 cups (500 mL).

   Since the kiwi looses its vibrant green color, green food coloring may be added. See photograph page 128.

Favorite Jam From Frozen Berries

In spite of the sugar being reduced, this recipe has always been a class favorite because of the fruity taste of the jam.

4 cups	frozen berries, any kind	1 L
1¾ oz. box	powdered pectin	57 g
1½ cups	sugar*	375 mL

1. Place berries in large casserole, cover and microwave on HIGH 5-7 minutes or until fully defrosted.
2. Add pectin to berries, stir well and microwave, uncovered on HIGH 6-8 minutes or until the berries reach a full rolling boil.
3. Add sugar and microwave another 6-8 minutes.**
4. Stir and ladle into sterilized jars. Yields about 4 cups (1 L) of fresh, fruity-tasting jam.

* Depending on the fruit, you may require more sugar, i.e. rhubarb is generally very tart so add an additional ½ cup (125 mL) of sugar.

** If mixture boils too rapidly before the end cooking time, REDUCE YOUR POWER LEVEL TO MEDIUM HIGH OR MEDIUM to prevent boil-over.

Red Currant Jelly

When red currants are in season, make your own jelly, or Red Currant Sauce, p. 103, for game or duck.

2 quarts	red currants, crushed	2	L
2 cups	sugar	500	mL
1 cup	water	250	mL
1 tbsp.	fresh lemon juice	15	mL
1 pkg.	powdered Certo	57	g

1. Crush the fruit and put it through a cheesecloth or strainer.
2. Add water and microwave 3-4 minutes or until mixture comes to a rolling boil.
3. Add remaining ingredients and microwave, uncovered, on HIGH for another 5-7 minutes. If mixture boils too rapidly, reduce power level to MEDIUM.
4. Pour jelly into sterilized jars, cool, and seal.

Yields approximately 3 cups.

Apricot Spread

19 oz.	can apricots, undrained	540	mL
½ cup	apricot nectar or fruit juice	125	mL
½ cup	sugar	125	mL
1¾ oz. pkg.	Slim Set	49.6	g

1. Place apricots, juice and sugar in food processor or blender and blend until smooth.
2. Microwave blended fruit on HIGH for 4 minutes.
3. Whisk in Slim Set and microwave an additional 4 minutes or until mixture boils.
4. Pour into sterilized jars.

Rhubarb/Strawberry Spread

2 cups	fresh or frozen rhubarb	500	mL
2 cups	fresh or frozen strawberries	500	mL
2 tbsp.	lemon juice	25	mL
2 tbsp.	plain gelatin (2 envelopes)	30	mL
1 cup	sugar*	250	mL

1. Place rhubarb in food processor and finely chop.
2. In large bowl combine rhubarb and strawberries. Microwave covered on HIGH 8-10 minutes or until rhubarb is tender.
3. Combine lemon juice and gelatin in a 1-cup (250 mL) measure and microwave on HIGH for 30 seconds.
4. Add gelatin and sweetener to fruit, and mix until blended. Microwave 2-3 minutes on HIGH or until mixture just comes to a boil.
5. Place in sterilized jars. Can be frozen or refrigerated for up to 2 weeks. Yields 2 cups (500 mL).

* For a low-calorie spread replace the 1 cup (250 mL) of sugar with 1 tbsp. (15 mL) liquid artificial sweetener, or enough artificial sweetener to taste.
See photograph page 128.

Cider Apple Chutney

7 lge.	apples, peeled, cored and finely chopped	7	
3 med.	onions, finely chopped	3	
1 cup	cider vinegar, divided	250	mL
1 cup	brown sugar	250	mL
½ cup	sultana raisins	125	mL
1 tbsp.	freshly grated ginger	15	mL
½ tsp.	crushed coriander seeds	2	mL
1 tsp.	dry mustard	5	mL

1. In a 2-quart (2 L) casserole, combine apples, onions and half the vinegar.
2. Microwave on HIGH 5-7 minutes or until tender.
3. Stir and add remaining ingredients and microwave on MEDIUM for an additional 20 minutes. Stir at least twice. Cool and pour into sterilized jars. Let flavors blend for 3-4 days before using.

Bombay Chutney

1 lb.	dates	500 g
2½ cups	white vinegar	625 mL
2 cups	cider vinegar	500 mL
½ cup	water	125 mL
2¼ cups	dark brown sugar	550 mL
1 lb.	cooking apples peeled, cored and diced	500 g
1 lb.	onions, diced	500 g
1 tsp.	cayenne pepper	5 mL
2 tsp.	ground ginger	10 mL
1 tsp.	dry mustard	5 mL

1. Combine dates, vinegars and water. Microwave in 3-quart (3 L) casserole 3-5 minutes or until the dates have softened enough to break into small chunks.

2. Add remaining ingredients and microwave on HIGH 5 minutes then on MEDIUM for an additional 20-25 minutes until apples and onions are soft. Stir twice during cooking. Cool and pour into sterilized jars. Let flavors blend 3-4 days before using.

Mom's Fruit Chili Sauce

A nice change from pickles with roast beef or chicken.

8 cups	fresh tomatoes, peeled and chopped	2	L
2 med.	onions, chopped	2	
2	peaches, peeled and chopped	2	
2	pears, peeled and chopped	2	
1	green pepper, chopped	1	
1	stalk celery, chopped	1	
2	apples, peeled and chopped	2	
1 cup	white vinegar	250	mL
1 tbsp.	salt	15	mL
6 oz. bag	mixed pickling spices	170	g
1 cup	sugar	250	mL

1. Combine above ingredients in a large microwave-safe bowl or simmer pot.
2. Microwave, uncovered, on HIGH 10-15 minutes or until mixture comes to a boil.
3. Reduce power to MEDIUM LOW OR LOW and microwave an additional 1½-2 hours to allow flavors to fully blend.
4. Pour into sterilized glass jars. Seal and store.
   Yields 7 cups.

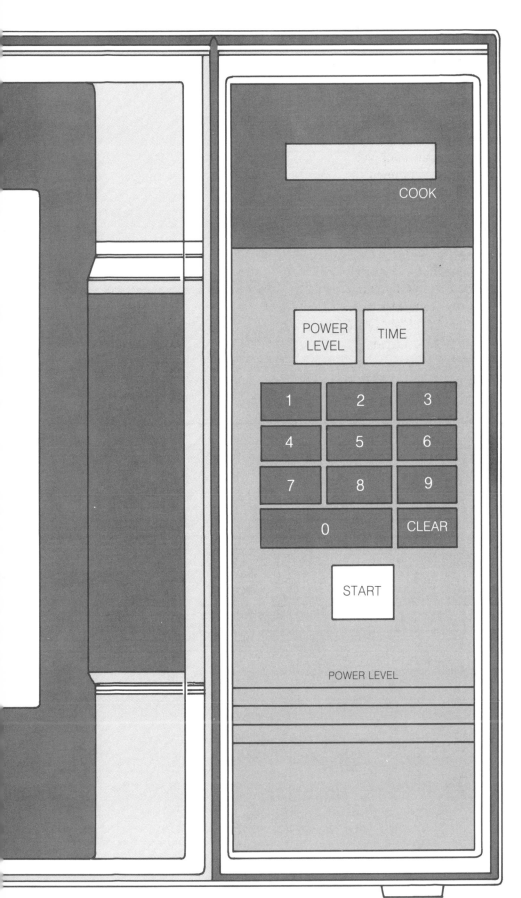

COOK

POWER LEVEL

TIME

1 2 3
4 5 6
7 8 9
0 CLEAR

START

POWER LEVEL

The Herb Garden

Herbs have become more popular than ever. They can be purchased fresh in supermarkets which gives us many new opportunities to try different things. Herbs enchance the flavors of many foods, especially when cooked in the microwave. We hope this information will help you to expand your culinary knowledge and you will try using herbs.

Basil or Sweet Basil

Predominantly used in Greek, French and Italian dishes. Tasty in soups, casseroles, pasta, rice dishes. It is especially nice with eggplant.

Cilantro — Chinese or Mexican parsley

This herb is becoming increasingly popular. It is the pungent leaf of the coriander plant. It is zestier than parsley so less is required. Great in soups, stews, and salads. Use sparingly. Dry just as you would parsley.

Chives

Can be used instead of onion and are reminiscent of garlic.

Dill

Excellent with sour cream, eggs, cream cheese, carrots and fish dishes.

Garlic

Good with a variety of beef, poultry, soups, stews.

Marjoram

Closely resembles oregano but sweeter and more delicate. Combined with other herbs, it tastes great in stuffings, eggplant, chutneys, meat and poultry.

Mint

Combines well with carrots, peas, new potatoes, tomatoes, lamb, green salads, soups, mint jellies, vinegars, yogurt and many other foods.

Parsley

This has high Vitamin C content. It is a popular herb and good in soups, sauces, vegetables, meat, poultry, egg dishes, and most popular as a garnish.

Rosemary

Has a pungent scent, excellent with pork, lamb, chicken, green beans, asparagus and tomatoes.

The Herb Garden (cont'd)

Sage

Good in stuffings, fish preparations, pork, goose, duck, Italian specialities, sausage and cheese dishes.

Savory

Adds a compelling aroma to green beans, peas, or lentil dishes. Great with mushrooms, soups, sauces, meats and preserves.

Shallot

A famous member of the onion family, but with a finer taste. Contains an ideal blend of spring onion and garlic. It has many culinary uses especially with fish, meat, poultry and sauces.

Spring Onions or Scallions

Common in Great Britain. Another delicate member of the onion family. Best when completely fresh. Used in peas, salads, egg dishes, cream cheese, mayonnaise and herb butter.

Tarragon

A fragile herb reminiscent in smell and taste to aniseed. Complementary to meat, poultry, mustard preserves and vinegar as well as sauces, especially Béarnaise. Use with discretion as this can be an extremely potent herb.

Thyme

A delicate warm fragrance, used in soups, sauces, fish, meats, vegetables, potatoes, marianades and preserves.

Watercress

A leafy herb used to add spice and zest to salads, soups, dips. Also used as a garnish. Store in a glass or bowl of water in the refrigerator or wash, shake off excess moisture and store in plastic bag in the refrigerator.

The Spice Rack

The flavor of spices seems to enchance foods, especially when cooked in the microwave!

Spices are more popular now than ever before. Low salt and special diets require spices and herbs which enhance the flavor of foods than cannot be salted.

Aniseed (Fennel, Finocchio)

A sweet-smelling, licorice-flavored herb used in liqueurs, cakes, over Italian dishes, meats, sweet pastry rolls, fish or just served as a vegetable. It can be purchased in most supermarkets, as a seed or as a vegetable which looks similar to celery.

Cardamom

A cool, eucalyptus-scented seed. Can be used to flavor sausages, pastries, or syrups. The seeds can be crushed and added to flavor coffee.

Cinnamon

One of the oldest, most popular spices. Some of the many uses are for cakes, pastries, chocolate, and beverages, such as coffee or hot chocolate. Cinnamon is frequently combined with other seasonings.

Cloves

Another spice that goes hand in hand with cinnamom. A pungent flavor used for ham, fruits, soups, sauces and cakes.

Coriander

A pleasantly sharp-flavored spice used in hors d'oeuvres, fish, sauces, soups, curries, and vegetables.

Caraway

A variety of culinary uses, such as Austrian specialities, cakes, breads, cheeses, soups, vegetables and some fish recipes.

Curry

Curry powder is a blend of several spices such as cardamom, cayenne, mace, fenugreek, white pepper, cloves, ginger and celery seed. It comes in varying degrees of heat. Curry goes well with chicken, rice, chutney, and coconut. Curry can be purchased in different strengths such as mild or "knock-your-socks-off" hot.

The Spice Rack (cont'd)

Ginger

This popular spice comes in root form or dry powdered. Either are tangy and even hot when used in large quantities. Ginger is used in several Chinese dishes, cakes and rice.

Mustard

Dry powdered mustard must be used sparingly as it is potent. It is used in sauces, meat dishes, hors d'oeuvres, and preserves.

Mace

A mild, fragrant spice resembling nutmeg. Popular in puddings, potato-based dishes, pastries and syrups.

Nutmeg

A pleasant, crisp and dry quality said to aid digestion. Eating less would also aid in digestion! Nutmeg is popular in cakes, puddings, pies, and quiche. It is freshest when purchased whole.

Peppercorns

Used to create a fresh pepper taste, they are commonly crushed or even cooked whole in meat, poultry and fish dishes.

Paprika

The most common 'browning aid' in any kind of cooking, paprika is red in color and very mild in flavor. It is used in soups, savory sauces, casseroles, on poultry, beef, potato and other vegetable preparations.

Notes

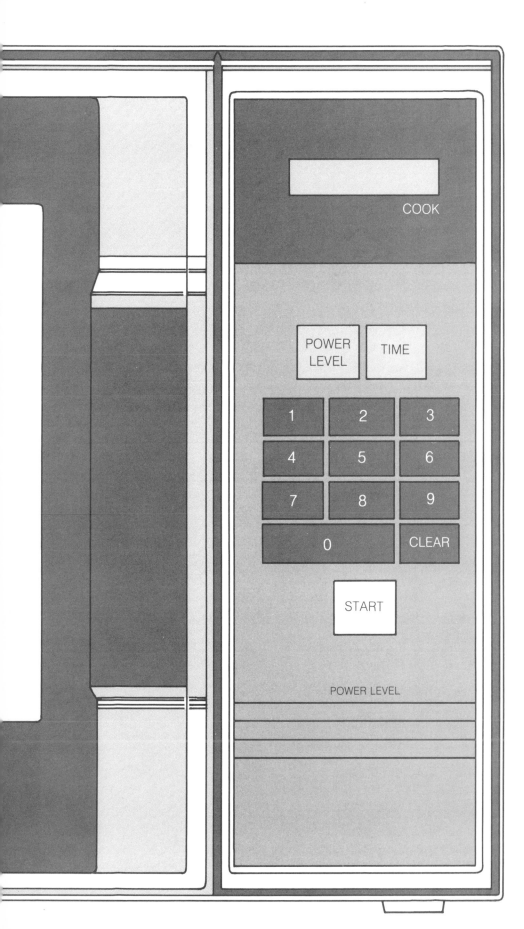

COOK

POWER LEVEL

TIME

1 2 3
4 5 6
7 8 9
0 CLEAR

START

POWER LEVEL

About Convection Ovens

We have chosen a few of our favorite Convection recipes which can also be baked in a conventional oven.

Use Your Convection Oven:

— just as you would your conventional oven. Convection cooking will be slightly faster, approximately 10 minutes per hour.

— for superior baked goods. The hot air flow aids in the browning and crisping of baked goods.

— in the summer to prevent your kitchen from overheating.

— to aid in last minute browning of some meats and poultry, etc. just after microwaving.

Note: Newer convection ovens on the market may have a higher wattage and therefore will cook faster.

THESE RECIPES CAN BE BAKED IN A CONVENTIONAL OVEN.

Cheesy Baked Potato Skins

4 large	baking potatoes	4	
¼ cup	corn oil	50	mL
4 tbsp.	grated Parmesan Cheese	60	mL
¼ cup	finely chopped green onions	50	mL
1 small	garlic clove, mashed	1	
⅛ tsp.	seasoning salt	1	mL
⅛ tsp.	pepper	1	mL
	paprika		
½ cup	grated Cheddar cheese	125	mL

1. Scrub potatoes, pierce and place them in a large casserole, cover and microwave on HIGH 12-14 minutes or until tender.
2. Slice the potatoes horizontally and remove as much pulp as possible without breaking the skin. Reserve the potatoes for other uses, see Thrifty Weiner Casserole page 64.
3. Combine the oil, Parmesan cheese, green onion, garlic, salt and pepper.
4. Place the potato skins, skin side up, on a cookie sheet and spread the oil mixture equally over top.
5. Bake for 15 minutes at 375°F (190°C). Sprinkle each potato with Cheddar cheese and return to the oven for another 5 minutes or until the cheese has completely melted.

Gail's Savory Short Rib Stew

2 lbs.	beef short ribs	1 kg
2 tbsp.	bacon drippings or oil	30 mL
2 cups	carrot coins	500 mL
1	small turnip, peeled and julienned	1
1 cup	chopped celery	250 mL
1 med.	onion, chopped	1 med.
4 cups	beef broth or water	1 L
5 ½ oz. can	tomato paste	156 mL
	salt and pepper to taste	
1 cup	water	250 mL
2 tbsp.	brown sugar	30 mL
2 tbsp.	vinegar	30 mL
14 oz. can	whole beets	398 mL
2 cups	chopped cabbage	500 mL
1 cup	sour cream	250 mL

1. Brown ribs in bacon drippings. Remove all excess fat from pan and add carrots, turnips, celery, onion, beef broth, tomato paste, and salt and pepper to taste.
2. Place in a 350°F (180°C) oven for 1½ hours.
3. Add remaining ingredients, except sour cream, stir and bake another 1½ hours or until vegetables are tender.
4. Place a dollop of sour cream over each serving.

Honey Baked Chicken Parts

4 lbs.	chicken parts	2 kg
1 cup	honey	250 mL
½ cup	soy sauce	125 mL
½ cup	chicken broth	125 mL
1 tbsp.	chili powder	15 mL

1. Arrange chicken parts in a large casserole and cover with the combined remaining ingredients.
2. Bake for 1 hour at 350°F (180°C) or until the chicken is tender.
3. If you wish to thicken the sauce, remove chicken from the pan and set aside, whisk 1 tbsp. (15 mL) corn starch into remaining drippings and microwave on HIGH 2-3 minutes or until nicely thickened.

Peachy Glazed Baked Ham

Peachy Glaze:

1 cup	peach jam	250 mL
¼ cup	white vinegar	50 mL
¼ cup	brown sugar, firmly packed	50 mL
1 tbsp.	prepared mustard	15 mL
¼ tsp.	powdered cloves	1 mL
4-6 lb.	ham shank	2-3 kg

1. In a large bowl or measuring cup, combine the ingredients for the glaze. Microwave, uncovered, on HIGH for 2 minutes or until the sugar has completely dissolved. Set aside.
2. Place the unglazed ham in the microwave, cover and microwave on MEDIUM HIGH for 12-14 minutes or until the ham is heated through. Drain off excess juices.
3. Preheat oven to 350°F (180°C). Pierce the ham with a sharp knife in several places and pour the glaze over top.
4. Bake the ham for 15-20 minutes or until it becomes golden brown and crispy.

Creamy Baked Fish Fillets

2 lbs.	sole or favorite fish, filleted	1 kg
¼ cup	melted butter or margarine	50 mL
½ tsp.	salt	2 mL
1 tsp.	dill	5 mL
1 tsp.	Tabasco sauce	5 mL
½ cup	grated Parmesan cheese	125 mL
1 cup	sour cream or yogurt	250 mL
½ cup	dried bread crumbs	125 mL

1. Generously grease a 2-quart (2 L) casserole with butter.
2. Place fish in the casserole and pour the ¼ cup (50 mL) of melted butter over top.
3. Combine remaining ingredients EXCEPT bread crumbs and spread evenly over the fish. Sprinkle bread crumbs on top. Bake, uncovered for 25-35 minutes at 350°F (180°C) or until fish flakes easily with a fork.

Hashbrown Casserole

2.2 lb. pkg.	hashbrowns, defrosted	1 kg
1¼ cups	grated Cheddar cheese	300 mL
¾ cup	sour cream	175 mL
1 cup	finely chopped onion	250 mL
10 oz. can	cream of mushroom soup	284 mL

1. Combine the above ingredients. Mix well together.
2. Place in a preheated oven at 350°F (180°C) for 40-50 minutes.

* If you do not have frozen hashbrowns, peel and grate enough potatoes to make 4 cups AFTER you have assembled the remaining ingredients. Pat potatoes with a paper towel to draw out excess moisture. Freshly grated potatoes turn brown quickly.

* For a variation and a complete meal, prebrown ½ lb. ground beef and place in the bottom of the casserole before adding the other ingredients.

Sherbet Macaroons

These tasty, toasty macaroons are a sure bet!

3 cups	coconut	750 mL
1 cup	orange sherbet, melted	250 mL
1	single-layer white cake mix	250 g
1 tbsp.	almond extract	15 mL
2	egg whites, stiffly beaten	2

1. Spread coconut out on a large platter. Microwave, uncovered, on HIGH 5-6 minutes or until coconut just begins to turn golden brown. Stir every minute. Set aside.
2. Place sherbet in large bowl and microwave 30-50 seconds or just long enough to soften.
3. Preheat oven to 350°F (180°C).
4. Combine coconut, melted sherbet and the cake mix in a large bowl. Fold in beaten egg whites. Drop the cookies by spoonfuls onto greased cookie sheets.
5. Bake 12-15 minutes in 350°F (180°C) oven. Yields approximately 30 cookies.
   See photograph page 160.

175

Gram Scarlett's Jubilee Jumbles

These pecan/date-filled cookies are topped with a creamy caramel icing. An old family favorite.

1 cup	chopped dates	250	mL
2 tbsp.	water	25	mL
½ cup	margarine, melted	125	mL
1 cup	brown sugar	250	mL
½ cup	white sugar	125	mL
2	eggs	2	
1 cup	Carnation evaporated milk	250	mL
1 tsp.	vanilla	5	mL
2¾ cups	flour	675	mL
1 tsp.	baking powder	5	mL
1 tsp.	salt	5	mL
½ cup	chopped pecans or walnuts	125	mL

1. Combine dates and water in small casserole, cover, and microwave on HIGH for 2-3 minutes or until dates are soft. Drain off any excess moisture and set aside.
2. Preheat convection or conventional oven to 350°F (190°C).
3. In another bowl add melted margarine, whisk in sugars, eggs, evaporated milk and vanilla. Add to combined dry ingredients. Fold in dates and nuts.
4. Drop by large spoonfuls on a greased cookie sheet and bake for 10-12 minutes or until golden brown in color.
5. While still warm ice with Creamy Caramel Frosting, below.

Creamy Caramel Frosting

The butter in this icing can be browned to give the icing a unique caramel flavor.

¼ cup	butter*	50	mL
2 cups	icing sugar or powdered sugar	500	mL
¼ cup	Carnation evaporated milk	50	mL
1 tsp.	lemon juice	5	mL

1. Place butter in a large bowl and microwave, uncovered, on HIGH 2-3 minutes or JUST until butter begins to turn a golden color. Watch carefully as it will easily burn.
2. Add icing sugar and evaporated milk. Beat with rotary beater until smooth. Adjust consistency by adding more milk if needed.

* In this recipe margarine cannot be substituted for the butter.

Rum 'n' Butter Cinnamon Buns

The special sauce in the bottom of the pan adds the perfect touch to these light and feathery sticky buns.

Buns:

2 pkg.	yeast	2
1 tbsp.	sugar	15 mL
½ cup	warm water	125 mL
3	eggs	3
½ cup	corn oil	125 mL
1¼ cups	sugar	300 mL
1 tbsp.	cinnamon	15 mL
1½ tsp.	salt	7 mL
3 cups	warm water	750 mL
10-11 cups	all-purpose flour	2.5 L
1½ cups	raisins, optional	375 mL
	brown sugar	
	cinnamon	

Rum 'n' Butter Sauce:

3 cups	dark brown sugar	750 mL
1¼ cups	milk	300 mL
2 tsp.	rum extract, OR	10 mL
1 tbsp.	amber rum	15 mL
½ cup	butter or margarine	125 mL

1. Combine yeast and sugar in a bowl and pour the ½ cup (125 mL) warm water over top. Let stand 10 minutes to activate.
2. In a large mixing bowl combine eggs, oil and sugar. Whisk until smooth. Add salt, cinnamon and the 3 cups (750 mL) of warm water. Whisk until blended.
3. Add yeast mixture to egg/oil mixture, stir until blended.
4. Add 8 cups (2 L) of flour, 2 cups (500 mL) at a time, stirring with a wooden spoon until the mixture is stiff enough to handle. Do not add all of the flour at this point. Cover the dough with a clean cloth and let the dough "rest" for 15 minutes. Wash out the mixing bowl and lightly grease it.
5. After the dough has rested, knead in the remaining flour (4-5 minutes) or add just enough flour to keep it from sticking. The dough will be ready when it is smooth and elastic.
6. Set your oven at 200°F (95°C) for 2 minutes or just long enough to take the chill from it.
7. Place the dough in the greased bowl, cover with a tea towel. Put the bowl in the warmed oven, keeping the door closed. Be sure to TURN THE OVEN OFF after warming it.
   Note: When using rapid rising yeast follow package instructions.

177

Rum 'n' Butter Cinnamon Buns (cont'd)

8. Prepare SAUCE by combining all sauce ingredients. Microwave, uncovered on HIGH 5 minutes, stir well. Microwave an additional 5 minutes on MEDIUM HIGH. Set aside.

9. Let dough rise 1½ hours or until double in bulk. Punch down and recover with tea towel.

10. Let dough rise another hour or until double in bulk. Punch down again and let rise a third time until double in bulk.

11. Divide the dough into quarters and roll out on a floured surface into the shape of a large rectangle ¼" (1 cm) thick.

12. Spread with softened butter, sprinkle with raisins, (optional) cinnamon and brown sugar and roll out into a long cylindrical roll. Cut at 2" (5 cm) intervals.

13. Prepare pans for baking by pouring ½ cup (125 mL) of syrup in the bottom of each 8 x 14" (20 x 35 cm) glass pan. If using 8 x 8" (20 x 20 cm) pans or pie plates pour ¼ cup (50 mL) of syrup in the bottom. Spread syrup to coat well. If you have remaining syrup left over you can use it on the top of the buns after they have come out of the oven.

14. Bake at 325°F (160°C) for 30-35 minutes or until buns are golden brown on top. Do not bake at a higher temperature or the sauce will burn.

Bake in Pyrex or ovenproof glass pans.
See photograph page 128

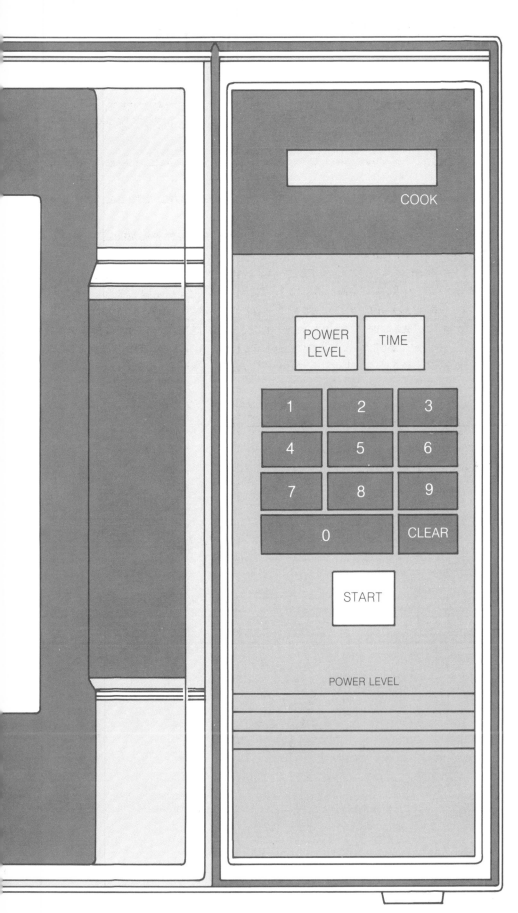

COOK

POWER LEVEL

TIME

1	2	3
4	5	6
7	8	9

0   CLEAR

START

POWER LEVEL

Crafty Ideas

Are you receiving full value from your microwave oven? Could you use it for additional purposes? Since we all want full value for our money, an additional "new concept" to microwave cooking is using play dough or baker's clay in plastic chocolate molds for more realistic shapes.

"I am not very artistic, you say". Well, you really don't need to be. With the aid of CHOCOLATE, SUGAR CANDY or even PLASTER OF PARIS MOLDS, you can create everything from magnetic refrigerator ornaments to baby wall hangings, as well as Christmas tree decorations.

This is an inexpensive craft which will enable you to spend many enjoyable hours with your children making your own creations.

See photograph page 128.

Play Dough Recipe

1½ cups	all-purpose or whole-wheat flour		375 mL
1 scant cup	salt	scant	250 mL
⅔ cup	very hot tap water		150 mL

1. Stir the flour with the salt until well combined.
2. Add the hot water, a little at a time, until you have a soft, pliable dough. For 2 or more colors, divide the dry ingredients and the water into equal proportions. Add desired amount of food coloring to each proportion of the water, then mix with the flour salt mixture.
3. Get ready to create!

    Items that would be helpful:
    — cookie cutters
    — toothpicks
    — garlic press to create hair
    — plastic magnetic tape (purchased at any craft shop)

    To seal and paint the dough you may use:
    — mod podge gloss (this is a glossy finish). Mod podge sealer and glue should be put on BEFORE the first coat of paint to seal the ornament.
    — water paints.
    — Testors paints for a high gloss finish.
    — felt pens
    — 1 egg yolk, divided into 4 portions and tinted with various colors of food coloring.

180

Magnetic Refrigerator Ornaments Using Chocolate Molds

Instructions for molds containing 8 to 12 fruit or animal molds.

1. Carefully press small amounts of play dough into the chocolate mold to ensure that the dough goes into each detail of the mold.
2. Fill the mold almost to the surface. DO NOT LET ANY DOUGH OVERFLOW. SMOOTH the dough carefully. You may need a dab of water to smooth out the rough spots.
3. Take approximately ½" (1 cm) of magnetic tape and gently press the sticky side into the dough. DO NOT PRESS THE TAPE TOO FAR DOWN INTO THE DOUGH otherwise the ornaments will not adhere to the refrigerator. Use more magnetic tape for the larger molds. (i.e. Santa faces, etc.)
4. Place the mold in the microwave and elevate, preferably on a shelf or inverted square casserole.
5. IMPORTANT — Microwave on your LOWEST POWER LEVEL for 2-3 minutes for each filled mold. DO NOT MICROWAVE ON HIGH as you will burn your mold.
6. To test for doneness, tap the mold, open-side down, on a cupboard and the ornaments will fall out. If some ornaments do not come out, microwave at 30 second intervals and repeat as indicated above.
7. If you wish to fill only ½ of the mold, microwave on LOW for 1-1½ minutes. If the molds tend to stick, spray lightly with a releasing agent before adding dough.

   If your oven tends to have HOT SPOTS, TURN AT LEAST 2 times per minute.

* REMEMBER, YOU ARE USING YOUR MOLDS only to form your dough. If you wish to continue drying the dough, do so without the mold. Even if the ornaments are not rock hard, they will continue to harden after they have completely cooled down. To dry ornaments that have come out of the mold, place on a large flat surface and microwave on low 1-½ minutes per 12 ornaments.

Completely cool the ornaments before painting or applying mod podge.

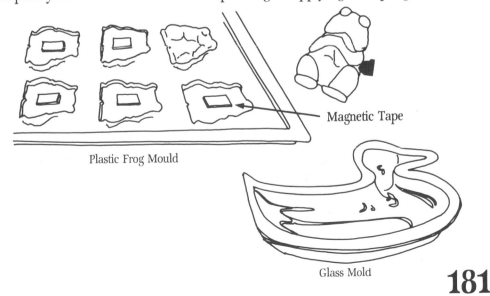

Magnetic Tape

Plastic Frog Mould

Glass Mold

181

Making Ornaments Without the Molds

See Play Dough recipe on page 180.

1. Form dough into desired shapes. It is best not to mold large thick items in excess of 3½" (8 cm) high by 2½" (5 cm) wide and ½" (1 cm) deep as the large thick shapes are difficult to dry evenly.
2. When making creations with cookie cutters, pierce the dough in several places with a fine needle to prevent bubbling. Roll each ornament to ⅛" (.5 cm) thickness.
3. Place 4 ornaments in a circle on a flat, elevated plate and microwave on LOW for 3-4 minutes. Slip a pancake turner under the ornaments and reposition them after 2 minutes of microwaving to prevent too much moisture buildup. If your ornaments require more drying, microwave at 1 minute intervals until moisture has disappeared from the surface of the ornament.
4. If your ornaments are beginning to get very hot, remove them from the microwave, cool completely and then microwave another 1-2 minutes per ornament.
5. Remember that these ornaments will continue to harden even after being painted.
6. If you wish to hang the ornament by a string, or on a wall, insert a fine hair pin at an angle into the back of the ornament. Do not let the hair pin touch the side of the microwave.

You can also use a wooden toothpick to bore a hole through the top of the ornament BEFORE you microwave, if you wish to thread a ribbon or string to hang the ornament after drying.

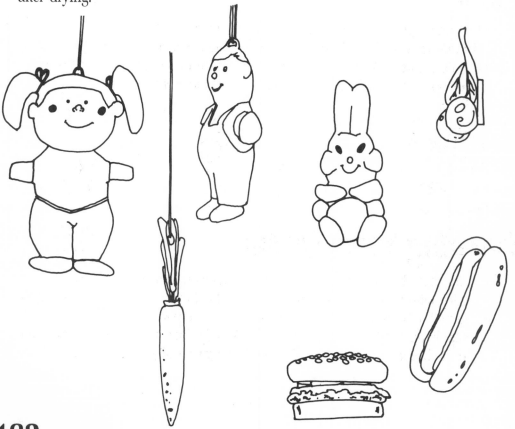

Directions for Creating Penny Panda

1. Roll out 4 portions of dough into balls approximately 2" (5 cm) in diameter. This will make 2 arms and 2 feet.
2. Roll out another portion of dough 4½" in diameter (12 cm) for the head, and one for the body, 6¼" (16 cm) in diameter.
3. Place the head, arms, body and legs on a flat surface in the approximate shape and secure the arms and legs to the body with wooden toothpicks. Secure the head to the body with another toothpick. You can place the arms on the sides or the front of the body, whichever you may prefer. Attach the feet to the bottom of the body or secure them into the top of the lower portions of the body. You may need to break the toothpicks in order to completely submerge them into the dough. ①
4. Form a nose by rolling out 2 small balls of dough about the size of the end of your little finger. Place 1 small ball on top of the other. Moisten with water to make the dough stick. ②
5. In the upper portion of the head, press an indentation on either side to shape ears outward. Use a paint brush to mold a neck.
6. At this point you can insert a fine hair pin. See note #6 on page 182. ③
7. Microwave 1 panda on LOW for 3-4 minutes.
   Microwave 2 pandas on LOW for 5-7 minutes.
   Microwave 4 pandas on LOW for 8-10 minutes.
8. Watch the drying process carefully and following the directions for drying ornaments on page 182.

Create any type of character you wish following the directions given above. Just remember to watch the drying carefully. If ornaments begin to scorch, remove from oven immediately. These ornaments do not have to be rock hard before painting. They do not chip when they are still slightly soft, and eventually dry out by themselves.

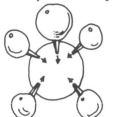 ①    ②    ③

Painting Your Crafts

1. As indicated above, completely cool the ornament, and paint the ornaments front and back with high gloss mod podge to seal the dough. Mod podge seals the dough and gives the ornaments a smoother surface before painting.
2. After applying a coat of mod podge and a coat of paint you may wish to apply another coat of mod podge or a coat of clear sealer to give a high gloss finish.

Index

Index

185

Index

Index

Index

It's Microwaved!

Please send me _____copies of **It's Microwaved!** at $12.^{95} per book plus $1.^{50} (total order) for mailing.

Enclosed is $_____.

Name: _____

Street: _____

City: _____ Province (State) _____

Postal Code (Zip Code) _____

Please make cheques payable to:
C & S Microwave Holdings Ltd.
3400 Cedarille Dr. S.W.
Calgary, Alberta, Canada T2W 5A9

Price is subject to change.

Treat Your Friends to

It's Microwaved!

Please send me _____copies of **It's Microwaved!** at $12.^{95} per book plus $1.^{50} (total order) for mailing.

Enclosed is $_____.

Name: _____

Street: _____

City: _____ Province (State) _____

Postal Code (Zip Code) _____

Please make cheques payable to:
C & S Microwave Holdings Ltd.
3400 Cedarille Dr. S.W.
Calgary, Alberta, Canada T2W 5A9

Price is subject to change.

Treat Your Friends to

It's Microwaved!

Please send me _____copies of **It's Microwaved!** at $12.^{95} per book plus $1.^{50} (total order) for mailing.

Enclosed is $_____.

Name: _____

Street: _____

City: _____ Province (State) _____

Postal Code (Zip Code) _____

Please make cheques payable to:
C & S Microwave Holdings Ltd.
3400 Cedarille Dr. S.W.
Calgary, Alberta, Canada T2W 5A9

Price is subject to change.

Treat Your Friends to

It's Microwaved!

Please send me _____copies of **It's Microwaved!** at $12.^{95} per book plus $1.^{50} (total order) for mailing.

Enclosed is $_____.

Name: _____

Street: _____

City: _____ Province (State) _____

Postal Code (Zip Code) _____

Please make cheques payable to:
C & S Microwave Holdings Ltd.
3400 Cedarille Dr. S.W.
Calgary, Alberta, Canada T2W 5A9

Price is subject to change.